Drive It
Forever

Other books by Bob Sikorsky:

- How to Get More Miles Per Gallon
- Every Driver's Guide to More Miles Per Gallon
- Break It In Right!
- Fools' Gold

Drive It Forever

Your Key to Long Automobile Life
UPDATED AND EXPANDED

ROBERT SIKORSKY

McGRAW-HILL PUBLISHING COMPANY
New York • St. Louis • San Francisco • Bogotá
Hamburg • Madrid • Mexico • Milan • Montreal
Paris • São Paulo • Tokyo • Toronto

First McGraw-Hill Edition, 1983
Updated and Expanded McGraw-Hill Paperback edition, 1989

ISBN 0-07-057522-3

89   FGRFGR   921

Library of Congress Cataloging in Publication Data

Sikorsky, Robert.
   Drive it forever.

   1. Automobiles—Maintenance and repair.   I. Title.
TL152.S523   1983   629.28'722   82-22904
ISBN 0-07-057522-3

Book design by Chris Simon

For Mom and Dad

Contents

The author acknowledges permission to quote material from the following:

St. Martin's Press, Inc. From *How to Get More Miles per Gallon*, by Robert Sikorsky.

McDonnell Douglas Corporation. From "Vehicular Energy Conservation Program," and "Improved Vehicle Efficiency," by Bob Allen.

Litton Educational Publishing, Inc. From *Motor Oils: Performance and Evaluation*, by William A. Gruse. © 1967 by Litton Educational Publishing, Inc., New York. Reprinted by permission of Van Nostrand Reinhold Company.

John Wiley and Sons, Inc. and Macmillan, London and Basingstoke. From *Fuel Economy of the Gasoline Engine*, by D. R. Blackmore and A. Thomas. Copyright © 1977. Reprinted by permission.

American Petroleum Institute. From API Publication No. 1509 and API Publication 1551.

Elsevier Scientific Publishing Company, Amsterdam, and Applied Science Publishers, Ltd. From *Lubrication and Lubricants*, by Eric R. Braithwaite.

The author would also like to thank the following:

The New York Times Syndication Sales Corporation for permission to reproduce in whole or in part a number of my syndicated columns.

Pennzoil Products Company

Champion Spark Plug Company

Chemical Specialties Company

Armor All Products Corporation

Ford Motor Company

General Motors Corporation

Chrysler Corporation

Society of Automotive Engineers

U.S. Department of Transportation, National Highway Traffic Safety Administration (NHTSA)

Introduction

This is a book that will show you how to get the maximum life and mileage from the major mechanical components of your car—the engine, transmission, and rear axle (differential)—and in doing so, also extend the life of other components.

It is a book that will show you how to extend the life and enhance the appearance of your car's paint, vinyl roof, vinyl dash, upholstery, and tires.

It is a book that will reveal current knowledge about body rust and steps you can take to prevent it.

It is a book that will give you up-to-date information on new automotive technology and how it affects the way you should care for your car.

It is a book for the car owner who is tired of being taken by unethical or incompetent mechanics.

It is a book for the car owner who is tired of his or her vehicle's wearing out after 80,000 miles.

It is a book that will show you *all* of the most important things you must do for the car to enjoy extended life.

It is a book for the owner tired of trading in his or her car every three years and never getting out from under the payments.

It is a book for those who cannot afford to buy a new car.

It is a book for those who can afford to buy a new car and want to keep it a long time.

It is a book for the owner who is perfectly content with her or his present car and wants to keep it a long time.

It is a book in which technical language has been translated into more understandable terms so *everyone* can benefit.

It is a book that will give you the very best and most up-to-date advice on automobile longevity and *show* you how to attain it.

It is, in short, a book for the car owner who wants to drive his or her car "forever."

A recent article in a popular magazine interviewed car owners whose cars had lasted at least 100,000 miles. These owners did not achieve these mileages by luck or chance, but by diligent attention to a number of factors, all of which will be discussed in this book—along with many more. They paid close attention to oil and filters, changing oil every 1,000 to 4,000 miles. They followed the owner's manual recommendations and in most cases exceeded the requirements. They kept their engines immaculate. They took care of the small problems as they arose. They had periodic tune-ups, either by a time or a mileage schedule, or, using gas mileage as an indicator, when the mileage fell below a certain figure. They weren't afraid to spend some money on upkeep, reasoning that it is better to pay a little now than a lot later. They all believed strongly in preventive maintenance.

The High Mileage Club

One of the regular features I run in my syndicated newspaper column is called the "High Mileage Club." I invite readers who own vehicles with over 100,000 miles to write and tell me about their cars or trucks and the methods they have used to attain high mileage. One condition must be met before a vehicle can qualify as a member of the club: It must have over 100,000 miles *without any major repairs*. That's important because in my mind that's the whole idea behind longevity driving: to get the car to last a long time without its being in the shop every month. Anyone can drive a car for 200,000 miles if the engine and transmission are rebuilt every 75,000 miles. There's no trick to that. But there is a trick to driving 200,000 miles without a *major* repair.

I've had readers tell me about cars with mileage ranging from 100,000 miles all the way up to the current High Mileage Club record of nearly 800,000 miles. Now that's making a car last.

How do most of them do it? By following the recommendations in this book. Many of the ideas contained herein are mentioned at one time or another by High Mileage Club members. You have the advantage of having *all* of these ideas between two covers. If the High-Milers can do it, so can you.

A car owner who follows the guidelines set forth in this book will find the 100,000-mile mark just one milepost in the automobile's life. How long *your* car will last will depend on a number of factors. The kind of car you drive is very important; some cars, given the exact same care and driven under the same conditions, will just last longer than others due to better factory design and material use. How you drive the car and under what road and climatic conditions have a major influence; for example, one car mentioned in the magazine article noted above ran up an astounding 1,000,000 miles—most of them while "on the road," not in city traffic. Close adherence to the "prevent and preserve" principles outlined herein will be your key to extended automobile life.

In 1987 consumers spent over $112 billion on new vehicles. Maintenance and repairs cost an additional $70 billion or more. For most people, the automobile is their second largest investment; the average price of a new car in 1988 topped the $14,000 mark for the first time. More and more wary consumers are fighting back against these high prices by keeping their cars for longer periods of time (seven plus years on average). The days of the yearly or every-other-year trade-in are probably gone forever. To avoid the big cash outlay, the consumer must protect and preserve what she or he now has. This is what this book is all about—showing the car owner how to protect this investment by practicing the principles of prevention and preservation. Every tip in this book will fall under one of these categories. Some tips will preserve more than others and some will prevent more than others; taken as a whole, they will combine to make one of the most powerful anti-wear remedies available to the car owner today.

A lot of things have changed in the automotive world since I wrote the original edition of *Drive It Forever* back in 1983. Cars are much better made today than they were back then, and they also are a lot more expensive. But their potential for going the distance has, in my opinion, been greatly enhanced. Even small four-cylinder automobiles can last a lifetime if the owner so desires. Better engineering and better materials, combined with modern technology, have been a boon for automotive consumers. Cars are a pleasure to drive again.

But modern technology has taken something away from the person who likes to do his or her own car servicing or tinkering. Almost every engine now is computer- or electronic-controlled. Fuel injection is rapidly replacing the carburetor. Electronic-controlled automatic transmissions, suspensions and emissions equipment, anti-lock braking systems (ABS), digital instrumentation, vastly superior and safer tires, variable-assist power steering, and even heads-up displays add to the growing list of technological improvements. And this is good, for modern cars are much safer and more efficient than their predecessors. Although this new technology has taken some things away from the do-it-yourselfers, they shouldn't fear, for there is still much the individual car owner can do to make a car last longer and perform more efficiently.

Although new technology controls the engine and transmission or transaxle, the basic units themselves remain and work much the same as they did in the past. Engines still need oil and coolant, transmissions still need fluid, and the car still needs care.

This new edition covers many of the things that didn't exist in 1983 and, in addition, updates and/or clarifies existing material. The new material covered includes: new high-detergent gasolines, ethanol- and methanol-enhanced fuels, fuel-injection systems and cleaners, the leaded gasoline phaseout and lead-substitute additives, 3-way catalytic converters, the problem of new-car rotten egg odor, the new API SG-rated oils, the hows and whys of oil consumption, modern cooling system maintenance, storing a car, choosing new tires, and much more. This book will, as did the original edition, give you every possible edge in fortifying your car—be it an older, leaded-gas-using model or a new fuel-injected, 24-valve, high-performance, double overhead cam wonder—against the premature deterioration and wear of the body, interior, engine, transmission, and mechanical parts.

1

The Engine Wears in More Ways Than One

Engine Wear

All automobile engines and other mechanical components of a car go through a three-stage life. When new, they are subject to a very high wear rate as parts mesh with each other and metal is shaved off until the parts find satisfactory mating surfaces. This initial stage of wear is relatively rapid but is nevertheless extremely important in determining the total life cycle of the involved parts. Once the parts have meshed properly, a zone of minimum friction is established; the mechanism, whether it be an engine, transmission, or differential, goes through a long period when measurable wear is almost nonexistent. Then at some point in this wear cycle, as even this slow wear takes its toll, the mechanism enters stage three and finally begins to wear rapidly and eventually fails.

The main thrust of this book is simply this: to delay the onset of stage three, the final wearing-out process that takes place in an engine, and to prolong stage two, the steady, slow rate of almost unnoticeable wear.

◊　◊　◊

One of the main reasons it is tough to get an average engine to last any appreciable amount of time is the built-in inefficiency of the engine itself. This isn't a knock against Detroit or Tokyo but is just a plain fact. Look at the following chart (Figure 1) to see how really inefficient the internal combustion engine is. At 55 mph, only about 25 percent of the total available horsepower is used to propel the vehicle and its accessories; the remainder is lost as rejected heat in one form or another. This is a very generous chart. Most estimates of internal combustion engine efficiency are closer to the 15 to 20 percent range. When being tested for emission controls in the U.S. government driving cycle, some engines have been found to be only about 10 percent efficient. This means that an astounding 90 percent of the available energy is rejected. If we can increase this efficiency, then engine life will increase in relation to the percentage of efficiency increase. Increasing engine efficiency is one of the goals of this book.

There are four main causes of engine wear: rusting, mechanical wear, corrosive wear (acids), and abrasive wear. If an engine wears out or a major mechanical component on your car fails, it is usually for one of the above reasons. In any engine, some of this wear *must* take place and there's nothing anyone can do to prevent it. However, much of the wear—in fact, the vast majority of it—is unnecessary and can be avoided. To learn how to fight this wear we should first become familiar with what it is. This section will familiarize the reader with the various wear processes and how they affect your engine. The remainder of the book will deal with ways of eliminating the *unnecessary* wear and delaying the onset of the unavoidable that will eventually claim any car.

Internal Engine Rusting

Internal engine rusting is caused by a number of conditions including climate, prolonged oil change intervals and/or poor-quality oil, frequent short trips, especially in cold weather, neglected pollution-control devices, owning an engine that is inherently more prone to rust than

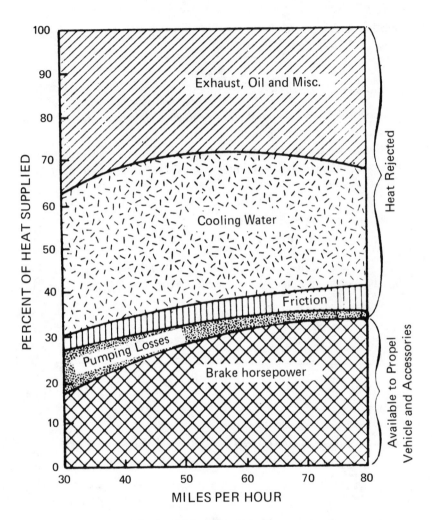

Figure 1. Available and rejected horsepower.*

* Notes begin on p. 205

another, and using leaded instead of unleaded gasoline. Let's examine each of these individually.

CLIMATIC CONDITIONS

Look at Figure 2 to see if you live in an area where internal engine rusting is most likely to occur. Chances are very good you live in a section of the country where climatic conditions favor rusting, because the area north of the dotted line includes about 90 percent of the U.S. car population.

PROLONGED OIL-CHANGE INTERVALS AND/OR POOR-QUALITY OIL

A very simple maxim applies here: The longer you keep the old oil in, the better the chances that rusting will occur. Engine parts are

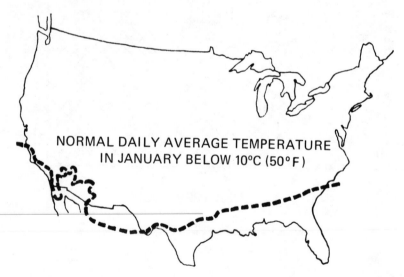

Figure 2. Areas of the United States where severe internal engine rusting can occur.

affected by the length between oil changes. You should be extra careful about how often you change the oil—especially if you reside in the area outlined in Figure 2.

The *quality* of the oil you use will also have a direct bearing on the amount of internal engine rusting. Some oils, due to the quality and amount of additives incorporated at the refinery, will prevent rust formation much better than others. Oil-change intervals and oil quality are discussed in detail in a later chapter.

Frequent Short Trips, Especially in Cold Weather

Studies have shown that rusting is most severe when the trip length is about four miles and the outside temperature is below 50°F. About half of all travel in the United States fits into this category.

Neglected Pollution-Control Devices

All newer cars equipped with EGR (exhaust gas recirculation) systems are more likely to experience internal engine rust than those without the systems. The moral here is that if your car has pollution-control devices, make certain they are clean and operating at peak efficiency. When malfunctioning they can rapidly invite rust and consequent engine deterioration.

Some Engines Are More Prone to Rust Than Others

Engineers have demonstrated that when tested under controlled conditions, some engine models begin to rust in about half the time it takes others. In some of these rust-prone models, chrome plating certain parts (lifters) helped reduce or eliminate lifter sticking and wear due to rust.

Use of Leaded vs. Unleaded Gasoline

Using unleaded gas instead of leaded will greatly *reduce* the chances of internal engine rusting. This is encouraging because almost all cars on the road are using unleaded fuel. These drivers should be aware that the extra 5 or 10 cents they may pay for a gallon of unleaded is money well spent as an insurance policy against engine rust. Not only will unleaded help rustproof your engine, it is also very effective in reducing or eliminating the problems associated with leaded gasolines, such as engine deposit buildup, sludge, and spark plug fouling.

From the above we see that the car owner can make the engine practically impervious to internal rust: Eliminate short trips on cold days or hold them to a minimum, use the best oil you can find, change it at the proper time or mileage interval, keep pollution-control devices clean and operating properly, use unleaded gasoline if the car calls for it—and, if you were fortunate enough when you bought the car, possess one of the engine models less prone to rust.

One study has shown that after the equivalent of 40,000 miles of engine operation, the mechanical wear, *when rusting and corrosion were controlled*, was too insignificant to be measured even by ultra-sophisticated methods.

Mechanical Wear

As an engine wears something very obvious is taking place inside it—the parts are continually decreasing in size. The parts are getting smaller because metal is being removed from their surfaces by either chemical or mechanical attack. Some parts, especially bearings, cams, pistons, and cylinders, are more affected by this process than others. In this section, let's take a look at the phenomenon of mechanical wear, that is, the actual removal of metal from one engine part by another. Whenever the engine is started we initiate the process of mechanical wear. Bob Allen, former Transportation Director of the McDonnell Douglas Corporation, gives the following excellent example of the wear process in a slide presentation and talk. In Figure 3 "we see a bearing in motion protected by a film of oil in the picture on the left. Six seconds after you turn off the engine, the film of oil collapses as shown in the picture on the right. The square designates an area that we will magnify ten thousand times." The three drawings in Figure 4 represent this area, magnified. Allen continues:

In these pictures the surfaces, which are actually smooth, look rough because of the high magnification. The lower surface is the bearing and the upper surface is the moving part. In the first picture on the left you see the film of oil protecting the surfaces by separating them. In the second picture, the engine was shut off and the film of oil collapsed. There is now metal-to-metal contact. When you next start the engine, you tear off the peaks of metal, which are then carried away in the oil. This is how a part is worn out.

Describing mechanical engine wear, Mr. Allen gives this startling example:

When you drive home at night and leave your car parked in front, it cools down. Later, when your wife tells you to put the car away for the night and you go out and start the engine, you accomplish the equivalent of 500 miles of wear as shown in this chart [Figure 5]. Ninety to ninety-five percent of the wear occurs in the first ten seconds in the start of an engine. If you merely drive the car into the garage, you still have driven the equivalent of 500 miles from the viewpoint of wear.

This kind of wear is *mechanical wear*, the actual removal of metal that occurs when engine parts are temporarily devoid of lubrication and metal meets metal. From the above example we see that it is

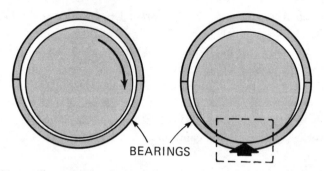

Figure 3. Bearing in motion (at left) shows oil-separating surfaces; bearing with engine shut off (right) shows metal-to-metal contact.

better to let the car sit rather than move it just a few yards. How many times have you been guilty of adding another 500 miles of wear to your car by moving it a fraction of that? Keep in mind that traveling on the highway with a warm engine and high-quality oil produces very little mechanical wear. It is during the start, especially the cold start, that most of the mechanical wear occurs.

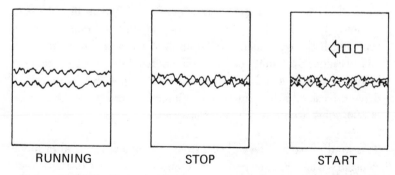

RUNNING   STOP   START

Figure 4. Polished bearing surfaces magnified approximately 10,000 times.

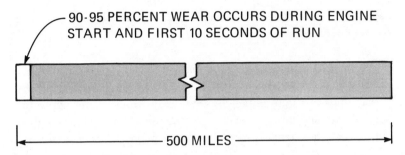

Figure 5. Wear during a cold start equals wear caused by 500 miles of warm-engine travel.

Corrosion—The Nasty Product of Engine "Acid Indigestion"

A friend of mine used to say that his engine got "indigestion." The longer the oil stayed in the crankcase, the worse the indigestion. At some pre-determined mileage he would take out a little jar, pour some fresh oil in it, mix in a couple tablespoons of baking soda, stir vigorously, and pour this concoction into his engine. He would then drive off with a smug and knowing look on his face. We thought he was crazy. But did he know something we didn't? He must have, for his cars always lasted a lot longer than any of ours and it wasn't long before he had all his friends dosing their engines with his formula for engine indigestion. What he knew was that the acid being produced in his engine from the combustion by-products was very harmful. He was aware that the longer the oil stayed in the car, the more concentrated the acid became. His solution? If it was not quite oil-change time, he would "douse" the acid with a couple of tablespoons of baking soda, just as you may do when you get a case of stomach acid indigestion. He was ahead of his time for he knew the damage just a small amount of acid could do, and he took what seemed to him the logical steps to prevent it.

For today's cars, acid is still one of the most—if not *the* most—

dangerous by-products of combustion; if not checked, it can start the corrosion process in your engine.

Every 100 gallons of gasoline that you burn, you produce 90 to 120 gallons of water and 3 to 10 gallons of unburned fuel. The quantities are determined by how much throttle you apply to accelerate and how efficiently your engine is operating. You also produce $\frac{1}{2}$ to 2 pounds of sludge, $\frac{1}{4}$ to 1 pound of resins and varnishes, which not only settle to the bottom but collect on valve stems and pistons. The combustion produces 1 to 5 pounds of nitrogen and sulfuric acids and 6 to 10 ounces of insoluble lead salts. *One of the most troublesome products is the 1 to 2 ounces of hydrochloric hydrobromic acid that is formed.* These acids will do far more damage than one would expect from such a small amount *unless they are boiled off in a fully warmed-up engine.*

Of that entire list of combustion by-products, the acid is probably the most engine-defeating product. How then can we fight this acid? We could do as my friend did many years ago and dose the engine with a shot of baking soda every so often, but that can hardly be recommended for today's engines (although it probably wouldn't hurt!). There is an easier way: High-quality engine oils are fortified with a built-in acid inhibitor that fights and neutralizes acid buildup—the oils have their own "engine indigestion" fighter built right in. But this acid-inhibitor additive doesn't last forever; it is constantly being depleted from the day you put fresh oil in. The rate of depletion depends solely on the type of driving you do and under what weather conditions you do it. Look at the Engine Wear vs. Operating Temperature chart (Figure 6) to see the accelerated wear that can occur in an engine when the acid-inhibitor additive in the oil is used up. With the acid inhibitor depleted, the engine wear rate at 100°F is six times greater than at 180°F. This in itself should be strong incentive for a car owner to be cautious about the oil-change interval and to use every method at his disposal to get the engine to operating temperature as fast as possible.

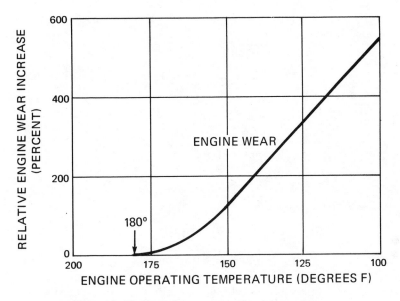

Figure 6. Engine wear vs. operating temperature.

Getting the engine to efficient operating temperature (thermostat temperature) is very important if contaminants are to be ejected and boiled out of the oil. Figure 7 demonstrates how contaminants, in the form of sludge, will accumulate rapidly—regardless of how fresh or superior the oil is—if the engine is not heated to efficient operating temperature *frequently*. It

shows the particles flowing into the oil when you start your engine. Note that if you drove only a few short miles, and the engine oil did not reach 135°F, the contaminants would condense in the oil pan as sludge. However, had the trip been long enough and the engine oil [been] heated up to 135°F or more, much of these contaminants would end up as vapor instead of sludge. On a day that the temperature is 50°F, roughly 5 miles is required to heat the engine oil to 135°F. Therefore, those of you that drive short

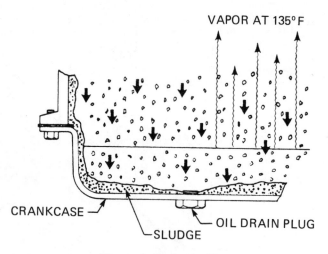

Figure 7. Sludge buildup.

trips of 5 miles or less not only are suffering poor fuel economy, but you are also adding to the oil contamination *with the consequent reduction of engine life.*

Thus it is very important for the engine to reach operating temperature, not only to run efficiently but to rid itself and the oil of contaminants. Corrosion-causing acids are one of the critical contaminants released to the air as vapor if the engine and the oil get hot enough. Many of the tips in this book will be concerned with ways to get the engine up to operating temperature as fast as possible and thus do away with the wear penalties the contaminants could inflict. We will cover specific ways that you, the car owner, can use to beat the problem of acid and the corrosive damage it can cause.

Abrasive Wear

So far we have seen three causes of engine wear: mechanical wear, rusting, and corrosive attack from acids. Let's now look into the fourth major cause of engine wear—abrasives.

Abrasive wear in an engine is caused when abrasive dirt, sand, grit, or hard oxide particles produced inside the engine work their way into the engine oil and are circulated throughout the engine, wearing on parts whose clearance is less than the size of the offending particles. *Abrasive wear is the most serious cause—and probably the most common, too—of engine wear.*

The best way to prevent abrasive wear is to eliminate the abrasives that cause the wear. The car owner should make certain his or her car has efficient filtration systems for fuel, oil, and air. These filters must be changed before they lose their effectiveness and allow abrasives to enter the engine system. The conscientious driver will also try to avoid situations that increase the possibility of abrasives' being drawn into the engine.

How do we exclude foreign matter? One excellent way is to stay off dirt roads and dirt parking areas. Figure 8 gives measurements of dust concentrations under different conditions. Study it and you may never take another dirt road again!

From Figure 8 we see that in normal air, the engine only draws in about .04 grams of dust per hour. Under dusty road conditions, however, the number takes a quantum leap to 86.7 grams per hour—2,168 times the "normal" amount. We all know how abrasive dust and dirt can be, so you be the judge: Is it really worth it or is it really necessary

ATMOSPHERE	DUST CONCENTRATION (MG PER 1,000 CU FT)	WEIGHT DRAWN INTO ENGINE* (GM/HR)
Normal air	5	0.04
Dusty road condition	10,000	86.7
Dust storm maximum for vehicle operation	40,000	347

*Engine of 6 cylinders, 216 cu in displacement, 2,500 rpm, 45 bhp.

Figure 8. Dust concentrations for various driving conditions.

to take that dusty road? Stay off dusty roads and don't park in dusty or dirty areas, and above all don't drive in dust or sand storms, and you will enhance manyfold your chances for extended engine and car life.

Figure 9 illustrates the actual measured rates of engine wear at various road dust concentrations. Most road dust contains about 70 percent silica, which is a highly abrasive substance, so it is not surprising that as the concentration of dust increases, the wear rate also increases.

It is obviously necessary to have an efficient engine filtering system. The system, however, is only as efficient as the filters, and the filter is only efficient when it is clean; its efficiency drops in proportion to the amount of dirt it contains. When buying oil or air filters (gasoline too), don't skimp; the best-quality filter is cheap insurance against abrasive wear of dust and silica. We will cover filtration systems in a later section.

Among the items that wear fastest in an engine—and therefore require clean, dirt-free oil—are the bearings. What do you think one of the main causes of bearing failure is? In an analysis of 4,000 case histories reported by a bearing manufacturer, the causes of failure were as follows:

Dirt	43.0%
Lack of lubrication	14.9
Wrong assembly	13.6
Overloading	8.4
Corrosion	4.7
Miscellaneous	5.4

No high-sounding technical names here, no tongue-tying chemical compounds to explain why the bearing has failed—just plain old common everyday *dirt*! An effective filtration system (coupled, of course, with good driving practices and maintenance procedures) is any car owner's first-line defense against abrasive wear.

CONCENTRATION (GM/1000 CU FT)	WEAR (MG/HR)
0.04	5
0.12	16
0.24	33

Figure 9. Dust concentrations vs. engine wear.

In this chapter we have looked at the four main causes of engine wear. Much of the remainder of this book is devoted to showing you ways this wear can be prevented. Most of the tips, from driving to maintenance, from additions to adjustments, will in some way prevent unnecessary engine, transmission and differential wear. Others will show you the most up to date methods of preserving the interior and exterior of the vehicle. Taken as a whole, they will guarantee the longest life possible from your car.

2

Driving and Parking Techniques That Prolong Car Life

A while back I was involved in making a video on how to find an honest, competent mechanic. One of the scenes called for a variety of cars and I volunteered my old high-mileage Volvo. I instructed the extra who would be driving it on the best way to start the car.

But when the director called "Action!" and the extra was supposed to move the car into camera range, he couldn't get it started. I could hear the starter motor grinding away and finally called a halt to the shooting so I could go and see what was wrong. The car had never failed to start for me. I got into the car, started it quickly, and the scene was reshot.

I'm bringing this up to emphasize a fact that many car owners ignore: As a car grows older, it won't act like it did when it was new. Yet many owners still treat their cars that way.

What's wrong with that? I hear you saying. Well, I don't mean you shouldn't be gentle and caring with your car, because you should. What I mean is that the working parts of many of its systems no longer fall within the manufacturer's specifications. Because of that, the recommended method that may have worked when the car was new may not be the best thing for the car now that it is older.

Let's go back to my car. The extra couldn't start it because he wasn't used to the car's idiosyncrasies. Even though I told him how to start it, he insisted on doing it his way, probably thinking I didn't know the correct method. And for sure, if he were to look at the recommended procedure in the owner's manual he could confirm that what I did was wrong. Yet years of experience with the car told me that the "correct" way just didn't work as well as my way, which turned out to be best for the car in its present high-mileage condition.

I'll bet you have a car that acts like mine. As soon as you let a stranger drive it, problems crop up. It's not your imagination, it really happens that way because the car isn't used to a new driver behind the wheel. Problems can occur in any number of the car's systems. That's why people who own trouble-free, high-mileage vehicles are usually the sole drivers of those vehicles. They "know" the car or truck: how it reacts, how it drives, how to start it on cold or warm days, what kind of gas and oil it likes, what highway speed it is most comfortable at, what kind of tires feel best and last longest, where to set the automatic or hand choke in different weather conditions and so on.

Listen to your car, pay attention to what it is telling you. It may be saying that you must pump the accelerator five times when it is cold rather than the one time recommended in the owner's manual; it may be saying that 65 mph is just a bit too fast and lowering your speed by 5 mph could keep it from burning oil and extra gasoline.

Let your car age gracefully. Don't demand from it the same things it could do when new. And don't be alarmed that it doesn't have the power or pep it once had. It doesn't matter as long as it still operates without compromising safety.

When I was a teenager in western Pennsylvania, a popular pastime among those fortunate enough to own cars or lucky enough to use the family car was to take the car out to a place called Three Mile Hill, get a running start at the hill, and see if the car had enough guts and power to make it over the top in high gear. Needless to say, many of those cars that did make it were pushed to the limit, straining to muster the power needed to get over the crest. Clattering valves and knocking engines were common sounds at the top. This is a classic example of lugging an engine, a practice that should be avoided at all costs. Fortunately, automatic transmissions can "read" the engine's needs and shift down accordingly, but a standard transmission depends on the driver to select the proper time to downshift. It is all too common for lugging to occur while going up hills with a standard transmission. The driver should always remember that it is better to be in a lower gear than straining the engine in a higher one. For prolonged engine life, it is important that you *never* "lug" an engine. This means that you should never overwork the engine in a higher gear when it can be shifted to a lower one. Trying to coax your car up and over that hill while in fourth gear can play havoc with even the best-conditioned engine. Lugging puts tremendous pressures on the upper cylinder areas and bearing surfaces; and besides straining them, it tends to squeeze the oil from between the surfaces, making matters even worse. This is where a vacuum gauge or tachometer is worth its weight in gold. When the vacuum reading falls below a certain range, or when the engine rpm's as indicated on the tachometer fall into a designated area, it's time to shift down and ease the strain. (See Chapter 7 on additions and add-ons for more about vacuum gauges and tachometers.)

Smooth, even, *minimum-braking driving* is a must. Try to learn to pace yourself so you can flow with the traffic. Anticipate and time stoplights so you arrive when the light is turning green, not red. Conserve what momentum you have built up; it costs you gas and engine and car wear to get the car back up to its original speed—don't do it all over again just because you are not paying attention to traffic. Drive "ahead," be aware of developing situations and take appropriate action to keep your car moving. Keep in mind that any time you use the brake, you are really "using up your car," because the acceleration process must be gone through again to get your car back up to driving speed. Try to get from point A to point B with the fewest stops and slowdowns possible. Keep that car cruising and your wallet won't take a bruising!

Drive behind the car, too! Use the side- and rear-view mirrors frequently to monitor situations in back and on each side of the car. This is superior safety driving and, by the same token, helps save the car and its fuel.

Are you a lane changer? Is it hard for you to stay in one lane? Do you move from lane to lane trying to get ahead of the crowd? Have you ever noticed that the guy who hasn't changed lanes at all is still right alongside you? Exasperating, isn't it? It doesn't pay to constantly swerve from lane to lane in the maddening, self-defeating race to be first at the stoplight. Lane changing costs you money. Extra gas is burned and the car suffers unnecessary wear, particularly in the suspension, steering, and brake areas. Pick a lane and stay with it as much as practicality dictates. Constant darting in and out of traffic will eventually take its toll in accelerated wear. Smooth, even driving is safer and far better.

Three-time world-champion race-car driver Jackie Stewart: "My overruling passion has always been to drive as spectacularly as I can in an unspectacular fashion." True professionals behind the wheel drive so that no one notices them. "Light is right," says Stewart, referring to a driver's touch on the accelerator and steering wheel. Those three words form an important key to extending the life of your car and getting maximum miles per gallon from it: It's right if it feels light.

Save gasoline and contribute to longer engine life by taking advantage of "right turn on red" laws. After stopping, if the way is clear, turn right on that red light and keep moving. Unnecessary idling time spent at red lights wastes your fuel and that of the cars behind you. Cut idle time and you cut carbon and sludge buildup. A good rule to remember is this: Less engine idle time = fewer engine deposits =

less engine wear. This rule becomes even more important when the engine is cold.

Ideally, an engine should never be idled above the manufacturer's designated warm and cold engine idle speeds. Revving an engine while the car is not moving *can only do harm*; it will never help. Except in a few special cases, such as when tuning the car, revving an idling engine to high speeds is a bad practice. Save those high rpm's for when the car is in gear and moving, or, as an automotive engineer would say, for when the car is under a "road load" condition.

This is especially meant for those drivers who like to give the engine an extra shot or two just prior to turning it off. Many people like to *vroooom vroooom* the engine just before putting it to bed. Don't do it, regardless of your motive. The old theory held that the extra revs pumped extra oil over the cylinder walls and made the next start easier. Actually, the opposite is true. Those high rpm's just before turning the engine off allow unburned fuel to dilute the oil, wash away protective cylinder coatings, and contribute to sludge buildup and oil contamination.

If Detroit made engines that didn't have to idle, we could put a huge dent in our national fuel consumption, cut down on pollutants, and reduce engine wear dramatically. Unfortunately, at this stage of our automotive technical development, we don't have such an animal. But we can do the next best thing to owning a no-idle engine—we can cut down on the amount of time spent idling.

Idling is a necessary evil. It doesn't do the owner or the engine one bit of good but it is still needed. Idling serves as an intermediate mode of engine operation and is necessary to usher the engine into a productive mode. How can we cut down on idling? There are numerous ways; a few will be covered here, and the reader should be able to add dozens more to the list. But first let's see how idling not only affects wear but also cuts into your gas mileage. In an earlier book I wrote that

EPA tests have shown that it is more economical to turn the engine off rather than let it idle if the idle time exceeds 30 seconds. In other words, if the car is going to idle longer than 30 seconds, you save gas by turning the engine off and then restarting it when ready. If the engine is going to idle *less* than 30 seconds, let it be, for it takes more gas to restart it than 30 seconds of idling will use. There are numerous occasions each day when gas could be saved this way: long stoplights, train crossings, freeway congestion, waiting in parking lots or in drive-in bank lines, to name a few. You probably can think of many others.

On the average, an engine will use about a gallon of gas for every 1–2 hours it idles. By using the above method you will accumulate good gas savings in short time. Remember the rule: Under 30 seconds, let it idle; over 30 seconds, turn it off.

Not only will this practice prove beneficial to your mileage rating, but it will also help reduce deposit buildup and wear directly attributable to prolonged engine idling.

Another good way to cut down on idling is not to start the engine in the first place. No, we're not being coy, just advocating that you make sure you are ready to go before turning the ignition. Starting the car and *then* remembering to light a cigarette or buckle the seat belt is bad economy. Always keep in mind that prolonged idling is considered one of the most severe engine operating conditions.

Automatic-transmission owners: Never shift your car into gear while the engine is at high rpm's. Your foot should be off the accelerator and the car idling at normal speed when the transmission is engaged.

Nothing will destroy an automatic transmission faster than subjecting it to abnormal internal heat. On a hot day in stop-and-go traffic, place the shift lever in neutral if you anticipate a stop longer than about 20 seconds. This gives the transmission a little breather and allows its internal parts to cool a bit. Just as a boxer appreciates those 1-minute breaks between rounds, so is your transmission thankful for those brief respites from the heat.

If the internal temperature of the transmission is below 180°F, its fluid can't circulate freely and the transmission pays a slight wear penalty until it fully warms up. But if it gets too warm, look out! Once the transmission fluid reaches 230°F, the life of the unit is dramatically shortened if it continues to operate. At a scalding 270°F you can expect an automatic transmission to last only half an hour! Think about that the next time you are stuck in traffic on a super-hot day—and place the shift lever in neutral.

Give your automatic transmission a little break by learning how to help it shift. Ease up slightly on the accelerator when you feel the transmission begin its shift. This increases engine vacuum and helps the transmission into a smooth, effortless shift.

On standard or manual-shift cars, get into the habit of always pushing in the clutch before starting the engine—regardless of whether the car is in gear. Besides being an obvious safety practice, holding the clutch in while starting the engine lets it turn over just a bit more easily, lessening the power required from the battery and starter motor, and making the whole act of starting more efficient. Many new-car owner's manuals recommend this practice for manual-shift cars.

◇ ◇ ◇

When stopped on a hill, always use your parking or foot brake to hold the car still. Don't hold it by applying gas to the accelerator, or, in the case of a standard transmission, by riding the clutch and applying gas. These dumb habits accelerate wear of the engine, clutch, and transmission. Use your brakes—that's what they're there for.

Use the air conditioner only when it is absolutely necessary—especially in city driving. Slow stop-and-go maneuvering with the AC on makes the engine work overtime. That same stop-and-go on a hot summer day qualifies for our super-severe service category of driving (more about this later). Rush-hour traffic in Phoenix in July is super-severe service. Being a desert dweller myself, I am well aware that this is exactly when you want your air conditioner, engine wear or no engine wear. Just remember that your oil and engine and transmission take a beating under these conditions and air conditioner use should be judicious.

On the open road the effect of the air conditioner is greatly minimized. In fact, using the AC on the road and turning the AC off and opening the windows for cooling are practically equivalent as far as fuel economy is concerned. The extra wind resistance generated by the open windows (the inside of your car acts much like a parachute) uses about as much gas as the AC would if it were on. The same tradeoff also applies to engine wear. Use the AC on the road—be selective with its use in town.

Any time you can avoid an unnecessary start, you save on engine wear. Make sure you have everything before locking the house door; otherwise you'll start the engine, remember what you forgot, turn the engine off (or perhaps worse, let it idle), go back in the house and retrieve the article, restart the car, and be on your way. A little foresight would have avoided that second start or idling time and thus some engine wear. There are many times each day when just a bit of commonsense planning can save you extra starts and extra wear.

Avoid sudden, fast accelerations. Slamming the pedal to the floor and bursting out of the starting blocks is always a no-win proposition for the car owner. Save those jackrabbit accelerations and sudden bursts of speed for the emergency situations that confront us all at one time or another. Fast accelerations, whether from a dead stop or while moving, will do nothing for your engine regardless of what they do for your ego. Bill Carroll, in his book *Tuning for Performance* says that some of the highest pressures inside an engine are encountered when the car is moving slowly and the accelerator is suddenly floored. Doing this places stress on all moving parts and lubricating oil, and demands every bit of power available in the gasoline (octane requirements are dramatically increased during sudden full-throttle accelerations). The gasoline that serves you well during routine driving may fall far short under sudden acceleration. Placing any engine under sudden heavy loads also tends to squeeze the oil out from between bearing surfaces, increasing the possibility of metal-to-metal contact and subsequent wear or possible engine seizure.

Have you ever noticed that the drivers who are always gunning their motors, taking off from stoplights like there was no tomorrow, racing from stop to stop, making their tires squeal, and in general "putting the pedal to the metal" are the very same ones who seem to be continually rebuilding their engines or transmissions in their backyards? 'Nuff said!

Relax. Be patient. Why the hurry? Many avoidable and sometimes dangerous maneuvers are done by non-thinking drivers in a hurry. Take it easy and save that car—and maybe your life too. Is that extra five minutes or so really going to make a difference?

Gears are tough but you can be tougher if you're not careful. Don't pop the clutch after coasting at moderate or high speeds; and, more important, never suddenly back off the accelerator pedal at high speeds. Both of these actions place extreme loads on the differential gear teeth (rear axle). If you have a habit of building up speed and then suddenly taking your foot off the accelerator and letting the car coast, don't do it. Smooth, even-paced driving is the rule. No fast ups or downs, unless it's really necessary.

Don't poke along in city driving. No, the slower you go doesn't mean the slower the car will wear. Actually, the opposite is true. Slow, turtle-like driving costs you miles per gallon and also increases engine deposits. Keep your city speed in the economy 35 to 45 mph range when possible. Most cars reach their maximum mileage potential in this range, so this practice not only insures top mpg's in the city but also promotes longer engine life.

Let's see how low temperatures and low speeds can affect engine deposit buildup. Talking about engine deposits, William Gruse, author of *Motor Oils*, notes that "Systematic work (in the author's laboratory) on the engine carbon problem at an early date showed that the amount of deposit was subject to a number of influences." He goes on to give three examples, one of which is:

engine running conditions, of which temperature was very important. The amount of deposit decreases as temperature rises; higher speed and load, which cause higher temperature, have the same effect. In a particular test unit, other conditions being constant, a change of head temperature, taken at an arbitrarily chosen point, reduced the deposit as follows:

TEMPERATURE	DEPOSIT IN GM/LITER OF OIL CONSUMED
171°C (340°F)	9.2
238°C (460°F)	6.0
351°C (665°F)	3.3

We see then that the warmer the temperature, the less chance there is for engine deposit formation. This poses a problem for the average driver as a majority of his driving is under conditions that do not permit the engine to warm up sufficiently (trips of five miles or less). This, of course, leaves the engine open to rapid deposit accumulation.

. . . in a clean engine, deposits will increase with time of running, up to an approximate equilibrium point, the rate depending on conditions. As more is accumulated and is effective in reducing conduction of heat away from the area, the deposit will begin to scale and spall off, to establish a level at which no more increase will occur; this value will fluctuate above and below a roughly steady value. A long, hot run under heavy load will break off some of the deposit, setting a lower equilibrium value for the new conditions.

Perhaps you've heard that taking the car out on the highway once in a while and giving it a "good run" is beneficial and will help blow out some of the deposits that have built up during city driving. This is exactly what is referred to in the above quote by "A long, hot run." It *is* a very good idea to get your car out on the highway periodically and to give the engine a chance to get fully warmed. The engine coolant must reach a temperature of around 135°F before sludge begins to be boiled off. If highway travel is not on your regular agenda, you should still make a point to get out and make that highway run. Surely there's a good truckstop where you can eat or have a cup of coffee, or perhaps a farmers' market where you can purchase fresh fruits and vegetables. Even once a month will help. Every trip you take that gives the engine a chance to warm fully is extra insurance against deposit and sludge buildup and the bad tidings they can bring if not held in check.

◇ ◇ ◇

"When Rolls-Royce and Bentley automobiles break, it is often because they are not driven enough. Routine service needs are often overlooked because the ultra-expensive luxury cars are generally driven very little." Those were the lead sentences in an *Automotive News* article called "Don't Let Rolls Sit Idle."

Owners think that because the vehicle isn't being used, it isn't wearing and therefore doesn't need servicing. It sounds logical, but it is convoluted logic. In reality, non-use can be as wear-intensive as driving the vehicle hard.

Remember the body/car analogy: If you don't use your body, it begins to atrophy, becomes weak and flabby, isn't as serviceable as it once was, and is more susceptible to disease and wear and tear. The same is true with your car, be it a Rolls or a Yugo.

Wear from non-use is a double-edged sword. If you don't use the car, you tend to forget about servicing it. That neglect then causes parts to wear more rapidly both when the car is used and when it is idle.

Don't use overdrive or fifth gear until the car has warmed up sufficiently—approximately ten minutes under normal driving and weather conditions. The rear axle and transmission fluids must be adequately warmed for these units to work properly and efficiently.

And while we're on the subject of warming things up before using them, here's a tip you audiophiles will appreciate. As I was road-testing a 1988 Chrysler New Yorker and listening to its Infinity sound system's "familiarization" tape, some good advice was passed my way. In cold weather, said the voice from Chrysler, it's wise to wait until the car's interior warms up before using the radio or cassette player. These units should be warm—especially the cassette player—before they are turned on. Being patient and allowing the heater to warm the interior will pay dividends in added life and efficiency from your expensive sound system—no matter what kind of car you drive.

The owner of a 1967 Mercedes received national attention when he drove his car over the million-mile mark—780,000 miles of it before needing any major engine work. One driving habit he followed religiously was to glance at his dash gauges every twenty seconds or so. Take a hint from a man who obviously knows how to get the most from his car—look at your dash gauges frequently; stop and correct any malfunction they may indicate. Dash gauges are sensors of your engine's condition—believe in them. Here are the four most common dash gauges or lights and what you should do in case one of them indicates a malfunction.

Oil Pressure Light or Gauge: This is the most important gauge. Stop immediately and turn off the engine if the light comes on or if the gauge shows any abnormal reading. Do not attempt to start the engine until the trouble has been remedied.

Ammeter Light or Gauge: Not really critical. If the light comes on or the gauge indicates discharge, get to the nearest service station or garage. You can safely drive short to moderate distances, but don't try to make it a long way, especially at night, because you are running on the power of the battery alone.

Engine Temperature Light or Gauge: Stop immediately. Let the engine cool down; add water or coolant if available. When the engine is cool, drive to the nearest source of help, keeping a keen eye on the gauge. If no water or coolant is available, you will probably be able to drive a few miles before the engine reaches an overheated condition. When this happens repeat the above process. Turn off the air conditioner and turn *on* the heater while driving; this will help dissipate some of the engine's heat.

Check Engine Light: You will have to go to your owner's manual to see what this light indicates for your car. It doesn't mean the same thing for all cars. It could be warning of an engine malfunction or may just be telling you it's time to have the engine serviced. In either case, *don't ignore the check engine light*, and don't drive with it on for any length of time until you know for sure what it means for your car.

Many auto supply stores sell a tandem unit consisting of an oil pressure gauge and ammeter. These are wise investments for the engine-conscious driver, for they indicate what is going on in the engine *at all times*, not just when there is trouble as the dash light would do. Combine these with an engine temperature gauge for maximum knowledge of engine conditions.

A warm engine should start *without* your pumping the accelerator. Any extra gas pumped into the engine will probably remain unburned: Some goes out of the exhaust and some remains in the engine, contributing to deposit buildup and oil dilution. If you have to pump the gas pedal to start your *warm* car, something is awry and should be looked into.

On most fuel-injected cars, no pumping of the accelerator is advised before either warm or cold starts. In fact, most owner's manuals advise keeping your foot off the accelerator while turning the key. Always check your owner's manual for both hot- and cold-engine starting procedures.

If at all possible, don't take your car on very short trips (five miles or less) on very cold days (below freezing). These are among the worst conditions the car can operate under, especially if it is parked outside and has cooled down to ambient (outside) temperature. If a bus is available—take it; if you can get the information you need over the phone—use it.

After a prolonged highway run, it's a good idea to let the engine idle a minute or two before turning it off. This is one exception to the less idling = less wear rule. There are a number of reasons why this is beneficial. Idling a hot engine before turning it off alleviates localized hot spots and helps distribute and dissipate excess heat. Sky-high un-der-hood temperatures are given a chance to normalize. This technique also helps prevent troublesome vapor lock when you attempt to restart the car.

If the engine is turbo-charged, after-hot-run idling will help the turbo return to more normal operating parameters. It won't suffer "heat soak," a condition that causes the oil in older turbos to "fry" and "coke" (to become like coke) and possibly damage the turbo.

How many car engines were ruined by driving in the ash- and dust-laden air caused by the Mt. St. Helens eruptions? Many car owners paid the price for trying to drive through this concentrated abrasive. Fortunately, you won't have to drive through the spume from volcanic eruptions during your everyday routine, but when you do encounter concentrated dust in the air, remember St. Helens: Pull off the road and turn your engine off. Abrasives (dust is one of them) can wear out an engine fast.

What is oil pressure and how important is it? The pressure shown on your dash oil gauge (if you have one) is the pressure at which the engine oil pump is operating, normally somewhere between 20 and 80 pounds with the engine warm. Actual pressure at other engine points is considerably higher and isn't measured by the gauge. What is normal pressure for your car? Consult the owner's manual—each engine is different and what is normal for one may be too high or too low for another. The owner's manual will tell you what is correct for your car.

It is important that oil pressure be at or near normal at all times. Without proper pressure, oil cannot reach vital lubrication areas and accelerated wear or engine seizure can occur. Continued use of an engine with abnormally low oil pressure can mean a very early demise for that engine. However, most oil pumps today are virtually foolproof and maintenance-free; they supply a constant stream of lubricating oil at all times. (Your best insurance of a properly functioning oil pump and correct oil pressure is to follow the oil change recommendations given elsewhere in this book.)

Try to park in paved areas. This applies at home, too—don't park in the alley when you can park on the paved front street. You'd be surprised how much dirt and dust can find their way into your car's engine compartment and engine when it is parked in dusty areas. Abrasive wear—that is, wear caused in the engine by grit, dust, and dirt—is one of the major causes of engine failure. Keep away from dirt- and dust-producing areas and you enhance your car's chances for longevity.

When parking your car long enough for the engine to cool down, always park in such a way as to make leaving as easy as possible. Example: Never park your car headed uphill. When you start it in the morning, when the engine is cold and lubrication is at its minimum, the last thing the engine needs is to have to put out extra power to pull the car up a hill. Instead, park on the other side of the street and aim the car downhill. There are numerous instances where a little common sense applied to where and how you park will pay handsome dividends.

When you come home after work, if you don't anticipate using the car again that day, pull it directly into the garage or parking place; park it in such a way that it is ready to go the next morning. By parking it *now* you avoid the wear penalty imposed when the engine is restarted later to pull it into the garage or parking spot. Although at first glance this may seem minor, it isn't; a substantial wear penalty is charged you every time you start a cold engine. (To see how much wear is caused by this unnecessary cold start, see Chapters 1 and 6.)

Always park the car in such a way that difficult maneuvers (turning, braking, and so on) are done while the engine is warm. There's no sense in making a cold engine work overtime when a warm one can do the same job more efficiently.

There are many instances each day when a driver can save gas just by parking a little sooner and walking a little further. Why cruise through parking lots time and time again trying to find a spot "up front" when there are plenty of empty spaces in the back? Take the first available space you see and don't be afraid to walk the extra 50 yards or so. . . . Slow stop-and-go driving is the most gas-consuming, so be willing to walk a little—you'll save a lot.

If the reader will take that quote and substitute the word "engine" for the word "gas," it will be just as valid.

Another reason to park further away and walk a bit more is that you are a lot less likely to get bumped or have a car door slammed into yours if you are in an area of fewer parked cars. The chances of losing a "chip off the old car" are minimized.

When parking in close quarters on relatively level surfaces, it is a good idea to place the car in neutral and apply the parking brake. In the event your car is "bumped," the transmission won't suffer any damage. In all other parking situations, place the lever in park and engage the parking brake.

It's always a good idea to engage the parking brake first and then place the shift lever in park or, in the case of manual transmissions, first or reverse gear. This action takes the load off the transmission and transfers it to the braking system.

Driving habits are different from driving patterns. Your driving patterns are the routes and roads you use most frequently in your daily rounds. Driving habits are the methods you use to get your car from one place to another. Although we are concerned mainly with driving habits, a review of your driving patterns can also prove valuable. Let's look at an example. Figure 10 demonstrates how most people drive in to pick up their mail at the local post office. Car B, heading north,

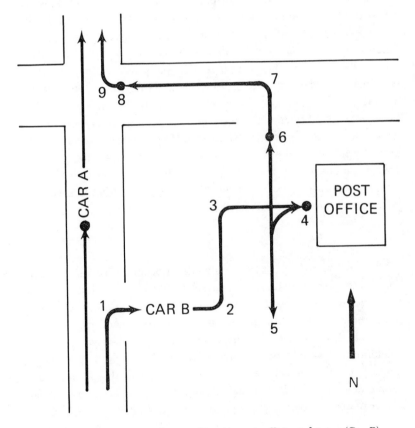

Figure 10. Efficient driving (Car A) vs. inefficient driving (Car B).

turns right into the post office parking lot, then must make a left turn to get into the main parking area. When a parking place is spotted, car B turns right and pulls into the parking spot. After finishing business car B backs out of the parking place, stops, and pulls forward to the stop sign at the north end of the parking lot. There car B makes a left turn and stops at another stop sign. When the way is clear, car B makes a right turn and is on its way. Total number of stops and turns needed to check mail: nine.

Now look at car A. The driver parks on the street at point A, walks across the lot to the post office, conducts business, walks back to the car and leaves. Number of stops and turns involved: one. Quite a difference when you consider that both cars accomplished the same thing—they went to the post office. The point here is that the other eight maneuvers of car B are unnecessary and cause unnecessary wear. Minor, you say? Not so. Over an extended period of time, say two or three years, it all begins to add up and take its toll. You can avoid this truly "unnecessary" wear by taking steps to prevent it now. There are probably many situations like this in your everyday driving patterns. Take a minute to stop and ask yourself if the maneuver is really necessary. In most cases it won't be, if you are just willing to give up a little convenience and walk a bit.

After you have driven a car for a while, it becomes like an old shoe. You feel comfortable with it and gradually get to know its idiosyncrasies. You acquire a "feel" for the car and know how it should drive, handle, and sound. Any time something out of the ordinary occurs, whether it be a clunk when you turn the wheels or a hiss when you press the accelerator, it should be an obvious signal that something is wrong somewhere. Unfamiliar noise is one of your signals that something is wrong; you should have it checked immediately, as it could be a harbinger of major repairs. Never put off investigating any unusual noise.

◇ ◇ ◇

Stay off dusty, dirt, sand, or gravel roads if you can. Besides playing havoc with the engine's filtration system, such roads can cut gas mileage considerably. Look at the following figures to see the difference road conditions have on fuel economy. Combine this fuel economy loss with the possible engine contamination that is likely to occur and you have excellent reasons to stay off inferior roads except when absolutely necessary.

This is a tough one, especially if you have teenagers in the family, but, if possible, try to limit the number of different drivers who use the car. It's much more difficult to make a car last if you have three or four different drivers, with three or four different driving styles, taking turns at the wheel. You may be very conscientious about how you drive, but the next person may negate all of your good input in one screeching jackrabbit start. Of course, having all the drivers in your household read this book may help considerably. Nevertheless, one driver is still the best formula for extended car life.

ROAD CONDITIONS:	MPG LOSS
Broken and patched asphalt	15%
Gravel	35
Dry sand	45

(Figures courtesy Environmental Protection Agency)

Figure 11. Effects of road conditions on gas mileage.

Oil—The Lifeblood of Your Car's Engine

The SAE Crankcase Oil Viscosity Classification System

Viscosity is the most important physical property of a motor oil. In cold weather it must permit the oil to flow freely and allow easy, minimal-wear starts and cold-engine operation. Yet at higher temperatures it must retain sufficient thickness or heaviness to ensure proper lubrication; it must not thin out and be squeezed from between the surfaces of moving parts, allowing metal-to-metal contact and possible engine seizure. All of this must be accomplished within the oil's designated viscosity number rating.

Viscosity is the measure of the thickness of the oil, or, to put it another way, it is the characteristic of the oil that determines how easily it will flow. The Society of Automotive Engineers (SAE) has devised a system to classify viscosities. An oil that flows very easily (thin or light oil) will have a *low* viscosity number, while one that flows like honey (thick or heavy oil) will have a *high* one. Let's look at the SAE viscosity classification system and learn what some of those numbers on top of the oil can mean.

The SAE system of classifying viscosities is a simple numerical one. Presently motor oil viscosities are broken into seven classes, ranging from the lightest or thinnest oil (SAE 0W) to the thickest or heaviest oil (SAE 60). In order these eleven are: SAE 0W, SAE 5W, SAE 10W, SAE 15W, SAE 20W, SAE 25W, SAE 20, SAE 30, SAE 40, SAE 50, and SAE 60.

The "W" affixed to the SAE number stands for "winter" and means that the oil is especially suited for use in colder temperatures. Oils without the "W" designation are for use at higher outside temperatures.

Your next question may be, What, then, are the multigrade oils and where do they fit into the picture? Multigrade oils are simply oils that can perform properly under both hot and cold temperatures. The discovery of an additive called a viscosity index improver (polymers) made possible the magic of having more than one viscosity grade in one oil. The presently available multigrade oils are: SAE 5W-20, SAE 5W-30, SAE 5W-40, SAE 10W-30, SAE 10W-40, SAE 10W-50, SAE 20W-40, and SAE 20W-50. As you can see, there is quite a selection. The main purpose of multigrading is to provide a light, readily flowing oil for easy cold starts, which then thickens as the engine becomes warm to provide higher viscosity protection at higher temperatures and engine loads. A multigrade oil is like having your cake and eating

LOWEST ATMOSPHERIC TEMPERATURE EXPECTED	SINGLE-GRADE OILS	MULTIGRADE OILS
32°F (0°C)	20, 20W, 30	10W-30, 10W-40, 10W-50 20W-40, 20W-50
0°F (−18°C)	10W	10W-30, 10W-40
Below 0°F (−18°C)	5W*	5W-20,* 5W-30, 5W-40

*SAE 5W and 5W-20 grade oils are not recommended for sustained high-speed driving.

It is important to understand that the SAE viscosity grade classification system identifies *only* viscosity and indicates *nothing* else about the type or quality of an oil or the service for which it is intended.

Figure 12. Guide to SAE grade of motor oil.

it too. A car owner who chooses an SAE 10W-40 oil gets the thinness and cold-weather 10W protection package, which ensures proper viscosity at low temperatures, and also gets the viscosity protection of a heavier 40-weight lubricant as the oil undergoes a transformation and thickens as the engine heats to running temperature. Which viscosity should you choose? The preceding chart will assist you in choosing the proper viscosity for your car. Use it as a basic guide when choosing your motor oil viscosity. (Conditions other than outside temperature that affect viscosity choice will be covered later in this chapter.)

A few things should be emphasized: *SAE 5W and 5W-20 grade oils are not recommended for sustained high-speed driving.* They do not have sufficient viscosity to protect the engine under high-speed loads and driving conditions. This is why it is very important to choose an oil with a higher viscosity (either single-grade or multigrade) when high-speed driving is anticipated. Bank robbers should always use a high viscosity for their getaways. Also note that SAE numbers identify viscosity only—nothing else. What, then, do those other numbers and letters on the can stand for?

The API Engine Service Classification System

Oils are put into separate classifications depending upon the type of service they are intended for; a small stationary engine operating under very mild conditions may require only an API service SB oil, whereas a new car must have all the protection provided by an API service SF or SG oil. Let's see how this additional classification system works and how important it is in choosing the proper oil for your car.

The letters API stand for the American Petroleum Institute, the group responsible for the formation of this classification system. Familiarity with the basics of this system and of the SAE Crankcase Oil Viscosity Classification System should give you all you need to know about how oils are classified and rated.

The American Petroleum Institute classifies oils by letters, each letter designating the type of engine or model-year car a particular oil is capable of servicing. If you glance at the top of a can of oil, you will see something written such as "API Service SG." This defines the "S" or "Service" category of that particular oil. The older categories are SA, SB, SC, SD, SE; the most recent, SF, and SG.

An SA-rated oil is at the bottom of the list, being essentially a straight mineral oil with nothing added. It should never be used in any automobile engine. It was originally meant for use in older engines that ran under very mild operating conditions.

SB oils have some additives to protect against scuffing, oil oxidation, and corrosion. A step above the SA oils, they still are used only under very mild engine operating conditions or when specified by the engine manufacturer. Remember when oils were called "detergent" or "nondetergent"? SA- and SB-rated oils are the original "nondetergent" oils.

SC-rated oils were introduced for use in the 1964 model-year cars. Their use was required to maintain warranty protection in all 1964 through 1967 cars. These were the first commercially available detergent oils.

Service category SD oils were meant for use in 1968 to 1970 cars and some trucks, and a few 1971 cars. These oils provided warranty protection for these model-year vehicles. They provide extra protection against engine deposits, wear, rust, and corrosion. SD oils fulfill the requirements of SC oils and provide additional protection to boot. They can be used wherever SC oils are called for.

SE oils provide warranty maintenance protection for some 1971 and all 1972 through 1979 model cars. Oils in this service rating provide additional engine protection when compared to SC and SD oils and may be used wherever SC or SD oils are recommended.

The SF classification was added in 1980. Oils meeting the SF specification provide warranty service for vehicles made between 1980 and 1988. These oils have better oxidation stability and anti-wear capabilities than the previous SE oils. They also provide protection against a host of other engine ills. SF oils can be used whenever SC, SD, or SE oils are called for.

The most recent additions to the oil hit parade are the SG oils, introduced in mid-1988. They provide warranty protection for cars operating under the manufacturer's recommended oil-change intervals for the 1989 model year to the present. When compared to SF oils, oils formulated to meet the SG service category provide improved control of engine deposits and enhanced oil-oxidation and engine-wear protection. They also give additional protection against internal engine rusting and corrosion. SG-rated oils are the royalty of the seven-member oil ratings family.

Again, just as with the previous categories, any oil meeting the API Service Category SG can be used in lieu of Service SF, SE, or SD oils.

There may be other lettering on the oilcan top. Perhaps it reads "API Service SG/CC." Any "C" or "Commercial" designation means that the oil can meet the commercial diesel engine requirements for fleet use, farming, and general commercial use. Here are the current API-recognized Commercial (C) or diesel engine service classifications.

CC-rated oils, introduced in 1961, are for use in naturally aspirated, turbocharged or supercharged diesel engines operated in moderate to severe duty service and certain heavy-duty gasoline engines. They give diesel engine protection against high-temperature deposits and bearing corrosion, and guard against rust, corrosion and low-temperature deposits in gasoline engines.

CD oils, introduced in 1955, provide additional diesel-engine-only protection against wear, bearing corrosion, high-temperature deposits and use of sulfur-laden fuels.

Rounding out the diesel, or "C" classifications, are CD-II and CE. CD-II indicates the oil is meant for use in severe-duty two-stroke cycle diesel engine service. CD-II oils also meet all performance requirements of API Service CD oils.

CE is the latest diesel engine service category. CE-rated oils are meant for use in turbocharged or supercharged heavy-duty diesel engines manufactured since 1983. They may also be used where CD oils are recommended.

However, any of these designations may also be found in combination with a gasoline-engine SG rating. For instance, an oil rated SG/CC meets the requirements for both API Service SG and API Service CC. Owners of diesel-engine cars will probably see a Service C oil recommended in their owner's manuals. But no matter what kind of engine your car has, gasoline or diesel, always choose the highest "S" rating —that is, SG—to be on the safe side.

The API Engine Service Classification System can be viewed as essentially a *qualitative* indexing of motor oils, the letters designating the quality and additive fortification package of the oil. An SA-rated oil, although of the highest quality and refinement, is far inferior to an SG-rated oil, the difference being in the additive package of the oil and the base stock from which both were refined. Of SA oils, the API says: "This category has no performance requirements and oils in this category should not be used in any engine unless specifically recommended by the equipment manufacturer." An SG oil, on the other hand, meets the most stringent requirements of the most modern gasoline automobile engines.

We should note, however, that API now considers the SA, SB, SC, SD, SE (as of January 1, 1989) CA and CB categories obsolete. They are no longer permitted in the service symbol donut. API says that "Use of the API service symbol will be restricted to current API Service Categories (SG, SF, CE, CD-II, CD, CC and/or any combinations thereof)." (See Figure 13)

Now we know what "SAE 10W-30, API Service SG" on the top of a can of oil means. But what about those other numbers and letters sometimes found on the can? A long number such as MIL-L-46152C is nothing more than a military designation for the same oil that is rated simply "SG." (Have you ever known the military to keep things simple?) We are concerned mainly with the "S"—"Service"—designations; the others (for our purposes) are strictly dressing on the can.

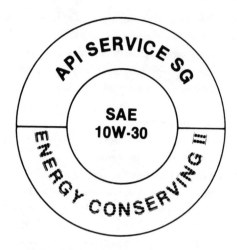

Figure 13. An example of the API Engine Oil Service classification symbol.

Choose an API Service SG motor oil regardless of your car's year, make, or model. Although SG oils are technically designated for cars of 1989 to present vintage, they are superior when used in older cars, too. An SG oil is superior to an SF oil (recommended for 1980 to 1988 automobiles) because it has extra anti-wear properties and better oxidation stability. This edge in additive content makes the SG oils wise choices. It is important to remember that although you can use an SG oil in place of any of the older category oils, you should never replace it with any oil of a lower designation (SA, SB, SC, SD, SE, SF).

If an oil is rated "API Service SF/SG," this means nothing more than that it meets the requirements of both categories of service. If they wanted to, oil manufacturers could label an SG oil as "SC/SD/SE/SF/SG," because the SG would fulfill the service requirements of all the other categories. We are concerned only with the highest service lettering on the can or bottle.

◊ ◊ ◊

A couple of things should be said about oils that have and those that don't have a desirable API "S" rating. There may be some lesser-known brands of oil that, in fact, meet the requirements for an SF or SG classification, but, because of the expense of the testing and approval process, the manufacturers of these brands have chosen to forgo formal approval and thus can't use the designation on the can or bottle.

On the flip side, some oils may carry an official SG rating but may not actually meet SG requirements. I know that sounds confusing, so let me explain.

It is strictly up to the marketer/packager to test and classify the oils he makes. At this writing there is no set of rules or formal procedures to adhere to when classifying an oil, and there is no separate independent body to submit the oil to for analysis and grading. According to API, "It is expected that his [the marketer/packager] knowledge of the performance characteristics of his product, including evidence of satisfactory performance in the engine tests . . . provide[s] the basis for proper API service letter designation." In other words, an honor system exists when it comes to grading and classifying oils. When you see the "SG" on a can of oil, you take the marketer/packager's word that the oil meets all the API requirements for the SG rating.

But some oils, when tested by independent organizations such as SAE, have been found to be unworthy of the ratings their labels proclaim. For that reason it may be wise to choose an established name brand of oil—one that has stood the test of time—instead of some Johnnie-come-lately that has impressive-sounding credentials. Although there has been movement to make oil testing and grading and classification a more standardized process under the auspices of a single organization, until that happens, it's still *caveat emptor*.

Better look twice at that can if you are buying oil at a quick service mart or food store. Many of these outlets sell only cheap brands of oil; on inspection of the can you may find it is only an SA- or SB-rated oil. This oil is practically worthless if you are driving a 1968 or newer model car. Unless you own an oil burner, stay away from these light-service oils.

Owners of cars with small four-cylinder engines should always be especially careful to use an SG-rated oil, regardless of what the owner's manual recommends. These high-rpm, high-load engines demand the added protection of the SG oils.

The Consumer's Edge: Oil Test and Inspection Data

The SAE and API ratings are the *basics* any car owner should be familiar with when choosing a motor oil for the car. This is the point where learning more about the oil is usually considered unnecessary, but for our purposes we must take it a step or two further and learn some things about the oil that are *not* printed on top of the can. This extra time spent will give you a decided edge in the quest for more miles from your car. In this section we will look into the *variance among oils within a designated service rating.* Even though Brand A and Brand B are both rated SG, one oil may have just met the minimum requirements for SG service while the other may have far exceeded them. You can't tell this by looking at the can. It's like comparing two baseball teams—they may both be good enough to play in the National League, but one can be a lot better than the other. Oils are no different.

One way to find out about the differences among oils within a service category is to compare their respective test specifications. If companies printed this information on the can, there would be no problem. But, although this data is not printed on the can, most oil companies are happy to fill a request for such information. Just write to the company address on the can and request "Typical Inspection Data" or "Typical Test Data" for the oil or oils you are interested in. Armed with this information, you'll be better able to make a decision on which oil suits you best. Don't be afraid to inquire about lesser-known brands, too— some may pleasantly surprise you. In fact, through this very inquiry process, we came up with a remarkable though expensive oil that on the strength of its test data seems to be far superior to most conventional oils. What follows is a sample "Test Data" sheet (Figure 14) similar to one you would receive from an oil company.

TYPICAL INSPECTION TESTS	FLYING HIGH OIL CORPORATION			
	10W-30	*10W-40*	*10W-50*	*20W-50*
Specific Gravity, 60°F	.877	.874	.873	.885
Viscosity, cSt @ 40°C (ASTM D445)	71.4	85.0	114	149
Viscosity, cSt @ 100°C (ASTM D445)	9.8	13.4	17.4	17.3
Viscosity, cP @ −18°C (ASTM D2602)	2300	2300	2300	9600
Viscosity Index	118	162	168	128
Flash Point, COC, °F	415	405	405	440
Fire Point, COC, °F	445	430	430	470
Pour Point, ASTM, °F	−30	−30	−30	−25
Sulfated Ash, % Wt., D874	0.75	0.75	0.75	0.75
Zinc, % Wt.	0.126	0.126	0.126	0.126
Calcium, % Wt.	0.169	0.169	0.169	0.169
Phosphorus, % Wt.	0.109	0.109	0.109	0.109
Sulfur, % Wt.	0.253	0.253	0.253	0.253
Color, ASTM D1500	4.5L	4.0D	4.0	5.0L
Total Base Number	7.1	7.1	7.1	7.1

Performance Level

API Service SF
API Service CC
  (except 10W-40, 10W-50)
MIL-L-46152, MIL-L-46152A,
  B (except 10W-40, 10W-50)
Ford ESE-M2C-153B
GM 6048M, 6049M
Chrysler Corporation

American Motors Corporation
European CCMC
Volkswagen 1302
Daimler-Benz OM616 Kombi
Fiat Preignition Test
Ford Cortina High
  Temperature Test

Figure 14. Typical inspection test data.

Once you receive the test data (you may be able to obtain it from a local distributor), the next step is comparing a number of the characteristics listed with those of other oils. Although there may be others, we want to compare just five: flash point, burn point, pour point, viscosity index (not the same as viscosity), and sulfated ash. Let's define these properties.

Flash Point: The temperature at which the oil will ignite. The higher the viscosity of an oil, the higher the flash point will be. This is an especially important property if your engine is burning oil. Paraffinic-base oils have a naturally higher flash point than do naphthenic-base oils.

Fire or Burn Point: The temperature at which the oil begins to burn off. Usually 20 to 30 degrees above the flash point. The higher the fire or burn point, the more resistant the oil is to burning.

Pour Point: The lowest temperature at which the oil will pour. This is important in very cold weather.

Viscosity Index: This is *not* the same as viscosity. It is a measure of how much the oil will change in viscosity as its temperature changes. A high viscosity index (VI) means the oil will lose or gain viscosity at a slower rate; a low VI means the viscosity will be altered more rapidly. Because we want an oil to retain its high viscosity and protective properties under hot engine conditions, a high viscosity index is a very desirable feature of any oil.

Sulfated Ash: The measure of the amount of unburnable material in the oil. A low sulfated ash percentage means there is less residue left as the oil is burned, and less residue means fewer engine deposits.

Although viscosities are comparable by merely looking at the can, this is such an important feature it should be singled out along with the above five properties. Viscosity, as we have seen, is the most important property of a motor oil. It tells us how thick or thin the oil is under certain temperature conditions. It has a direct bearing on the amount of heat generated by an engine, how much oil it uses or loses, how good the compression is, and how easily the car will start, particularly in cold weather. Keep these properties in mind, for we will return to them.

Additives in Your Oil

What is the purpose of a motor oil? To lubricate the engine, you answer, what else? Actually this is only one function of a modern motor oil—it has many more, as we shall see.

Most modern motor oils have a list of functions to perform that make them seem like an automotive Houdini. A high-quality oil should allow for easy starts, lubricate the engine under all modes of operation, reduce friction and the wear it causes, guard against rust and corrosion, keep the internal engine parts sparkling clean, reduce or even eliminate engine deposits and buildup, act as the primary coolant for many engine parts, provide a good seal in the cylinders so that proper efficient combustion can take place, and, last but not least, be non-foaming.

To be successful in accomplishing the above goals, modern motor oils have incorporated a performance additive package. Additives are chemicals that are blended with the base stock mineral oil and impart to it specially desired properties. The additive amount can vary from less than 1 percent to over 33 percent of the total volume of the oil. No two companies will come up with the exact same proportion of additives, and some differ remarkably in amount and type of additives included. This is one of the reasons all oils are not the same. Following are some of the more common additives found in modern motor oils.

Viscosity Index Improvers: Chemicals that make possible the multigrade oils we have today. They increase the viscosity of the oil at high temperatures (thicken it) and keep it less viscous (free flowing) at low temperatures.

Anti-foam Agents: These prevent the oil from foaming. The amount an oil will foam in its natural state depends on where it is from, what viscosity it is, and how refined it is.

Detergents and Dispersants: Detergents neutralize deposits before they can do any harm; dispersants keep contaminants suspended in the oil and prevent them from agglomerating into sludge. All oils today, except SA- and SB-rated ones, are detergent oils.

Rust Inhibitors: By bonding a protective film to metal surfaces, these additives prevent water from attacking and causing rust.

Corrosion Inhibitors: These prevent corrosion from acids and other contaminants in the oil. Zinc is a commonly used corrosion fighter.

Oxidation Inhibitors: Prevent oil oxidation at high temperatures. Oil oxidation can cause an increase in acids and encourage gum, varnish, and lacquer deposits to form.

Pour-point Depressants: Chemicals that prevent or slow the formation of wax crystals at low temperatures. They prevent your oil from becoming a mass of unyielding glop at low temperatures.

Anti-wear Additives: These reduce friction and wear under milder conditions of engine operation.

EP or Extreme Pressure Additives: Anti-wear additives that are effective at high temperatures or under heavy engine loading. They form tough films on the metal surfaces that prevent metal-to-metal contact.

We see now that oil isn't just oil but a complex blending of additives and base stock mineral oils that meet each company's particular specifications. As with any product, one company will make a better one than the next, and by comparing test information and additive content (if available), you are much better prepared to choose the motor oil that is best suited to your driving needs. For instance, if you often drive in very cold weather, a low *pour point* will be of interest to you. If your car is using too much oil, perhaps your current oil is burning off too easily; changing to an oil with a *higher flash point* may cure the problem. A *low sulfated ash* content is desirable under all driving conditions for it means less unburned materials to pollute the engine. A *high viscosity index* means the oil will maintain its viscosity under high loads and temperatures for a longer time and won't break down under these demanding conditions. The higher the viscosity index, the better the oil will resist wear in the engine.

When comparing oil test data, the following properties are, in general, considered desirable: *HIGH* flash and burn points; *LOW* pour point, especially in cold climates; *LOW* sulfated ash content; *HIGH* viscosity index. Viscosity itself should be chosen in accordance with the manufacturer's recommendations for the type of driving you do and the weather you do it in.

Another "test data" sheet reads as follows for the properties we are most interested in:

SAE	10W-30	10W-40	20W-50
Viscosity Index	130	145	125
Flash Point	410	410	430
Pour Point	−25	−25	−10
Sulfated Ash	1.00	1.00	1.00

When compared to the prior test data, we see that the two products are fairly similar in flash points, but the first oil is superior in the remaining properties. Also, the second oil company doesn't offer a 10W-50 viscosity, which may be exactly what you are looking for. These two test data comparisons were taken from two popular brands of oil now on the market. As you can see, it pays to shop around.

Although test data is a useful comparison tool, it should never be the final word in choosing a motor oil. The test data may single out a number of motor oils you will want to compare. High and low numbers are excellent reference and starting points, but in the final analysis it's how well the oil works in your engine that should be the determining factor. The proof of this pudding is in the engine.

Oil Consumption—Just How Much Is "Normal"

In a syndicated column I discussed the mystery of the missing oil:

You've got this mysterious problem with your car and can't figure out what's causing it. You've asked 10 people and received 10 different answers. It's really bugging you, so you drop me a line. A number of you, with exactly the same problem, have done just that. I can see why it has baffled both novice and mechanic alike.

Your car never used oil. You change it regularly every 3,000 miles or so. The car is seldom driven at high speeds, and is used almost exclusively for in-town chores. A lot of slow stop-and-go coupled with extensive periods of idling is typical.

So you decide to take the old buggy out for a spin. Blow some carbon out of the engine and give it a little run at the legal limit. After an hour or two of highway driving you stop, get gas and ask the attendant to check the oil. To your amazement it turns out to be 2 quarts low. That can't be, you think, this car doesn't use oil. You check it yourself. Yep, 2 quarts low and you've only gone about 100 miles.

You replace the missing oil and drive back to town, apprehensive about checking the oil level for fear it will be 2 quarts low again. Something must have happened to the engine during the trip to cause the car to use that much oil. But when you check, lo and behold, the oil is up to the full mark. What in the world is going on?

The answer lies in your suspicion that something during the trip caused the car to use oil. You're right, but for the wrong reasons. Although you never knew it, your car has always used oil, but its usage was never evident because the crankcase was replenished with—no, not oil—unburned fuel and other combustion by-products. This not only diluted the oil in the crankcase, but also made it appear full.

Your city-only driving continued to accrue lots of unburned fuel and never provided the opportunity for the contaminants to burn off. When you took the car out on the highway and got it going 65 mph for an extended period, the volatile contaminants were, for the first time, heated to a high enough temperature to boil off. What happened? Bingo! The quarts of "false oil" were gone before you could say "Robinson Crusoe." The highly diluted oil, quite thin and low in viscosity, had little resistance to the rigors of high-speed driving and was rapidly used up.

Why didn't another 2 quarts boil off on the return trip? Because by then most of the volatile contaminants had boiled off, and the 2 fresh quarts you added were providing true protection. Fresh oil is not as easily burned off as the volatile hydrocarbons that had accumulated.

Add to this the fact that high-speed driving will burn oil much faster than slow driving and you have the reasons why your car suddenly began to use oil. Remember that a gasoline engine can use up to seven times the amount of engine oil at 70 mph as it uses at 40 mph.

Best advice here is to change the oil more frequently when doing in-town-only driving. Always change it before a trip. Try upping the viscosity by at least 10 numbers; if you are using 10W-30 for city driving, change it to 10W-40 for that highway trip.

Oil Consumption Isn't Always Related to Engine Wear

Most car owners—and mechanics, too—have traditionally used oil consumption as a yardstick of how the engine is wearing. The more oil it uses, the closer it comes to being a candidate for rebuilding or becoming a resident of that great salvage yard over yonder.

But a recent study, using a new instrument called an SO2 micro-coulometer, has shed light on the subject of oil consumption, demonstrating that it may not always be related to engine wear, but could be a function of other variables. Everyone is interested in why his or her car uses oil, so let's take a look at what this high-tech gadget has uncovered and how the data can benefit us.

For the experiments a commercial 10W-30 oil was used in a Ford 1.6-liter, in-line, four-cylinder overhead cam engine with an 8.8:1 compression ratio. A technical-grade fuel was used to keep the sulfur in the exhaust consistent. (The microcoulometer measures the total amount of oil consumption by calculating the amount of sulfur in the exhaust.) No, you can't buy this fuel at the pump.

The SAE study "Real-Time Oil Consumption Measurement" notes that there are two types of engine oil consumption: chemical loss and physical loss. Chemical loss occurs when the oil is burned; physical loss occurs "when the engine oil is transported from the engine as an uncombusted vapor which, downstream in the exhaust system, may nucleate to form oil aerosol." Oil aerosol is like a fine mist or spray.

The tests were conducted at two engine-operating conditions, one at 1,750 rpm and the other at 3,500 rpm—wide-open throttle. At 1,750 rpm (which would be gently cruising for most four-cylinder cars) oil consumption was measured at 0.59 quarts per 10,000 miles; at 3,500 rpm it jumped significantly to 1.42 quarts per 10,000 miles. The lesson here is clear for everyday drivers: The faster you go, the more oil your car uses. You don't need a microcoulometer to find that out.

However, there is more to it than that. Engine temperature plays an important role. For the engine operated at 1,750 rpm, temperature was held at 204°F and oil consumption was measured at 0.56 quarts per 10,000 miles, almost identical to the 0.59 quarts noted above. But when the water (coolant) temperature was lowered to 182°F, oil consumption decreased to 0.39 quarts per 10,000 miles. The lesson here is that oil consumption seems to rise with an increase in coolant/water temperature—a cooler engine uses less oil. But remember that when you drive faster, the engine usually runs hotter, so both mechanisms —higher temperature and engine speed—combine to make your car use more oil.

These experiments also confirmed what many chemists and oil engineers have known for a long time: When new oil is put into an engine—especially when you switch from one brand to another—the initial oil consumption can be quite high because fresh oil contains highly volatile substances that burn off rapidly.

The study concluded that "the initial 60 minutes of engine operation following an oil change is not representative of the level of long-term oil consumption and may be a strong function of the type and source of oil." Lesson for everyday drivers: If your car is using oil, it may be the fault of the oil, not the engine. Give the oil a chance. Most oil consumption will occur in the first five hours of driving after an oil change. If you are switching brands of oil, don't make a decision until after two oil changes.

Another interesting fact the study brought out is how the PCV (positive crankcase ventilation) valve affects oil consumption. When the PCV valve was bypassed or disconnected, oil consumption decreased; when it was active, oil consumption increased. When the restriction was varied, oil consumption varied. This isn't to say that you should fool with your PCV, because you shouldn't. You may burn less oil without one, but the amount of pollutants you substitute for the unburned oil isn't a fair trade-off.

The minimum acceptable flash point that will prevent oil from just burning away is around 200°C (392°F). It is rare to find a flash point that low anymore, but be sure to check those numbers carefully if the oil you are presently using is being burned off rapidly.

If your engine is using oil and you're puzzled as to the cause, slide a large piece of cardboard under the front engine compartment when you park the car for the night. If there is a leak, this will show you the general vicinity. If the cardboard is free of drippings, place it under the car again when the engine is warm and running. If it is still dry, then your problem probably is not a leak; your engine is using oil internally. *If the oil use is not excessive,* this is a good time to determine whether changing to a different *brand* might reduce consumption. Try switching to an oil with a higher flash point than the one you are now using. If your current oil has a flash point of 400, then switch to one with a rating of 450 or so. A higher flash point can, in many cases, help reduce or even stop oil consumption. Flash points can also vary within the same brand of oil—the higher the viscosity, the higher the flash point. This is why switching to a higher viscosity oil can also be effective in reducing oil consumption. When switching brands, also go up a notch in viscosity over your present brand. If you have been using an SAE 20 oil with a flash point of 400 and note that Brand B SAE 20 oil has a flash point of 450, switch to that brand and at the same time go up a notch in viscosity, to SAE 30. Moving from a 20 weight to a 30 weight will contribute to the flash point by another 10 degrees or more. Brand B SAE 30 oil will have a flash point of around 460, an increase of 60 over the original oil. Hopefully, this will cure or reduce the oil consumption problem.

A less viscous oil (low viscosity) tends to vaporize more easily than a more viscous one, therefore you can expect to use a bit more oil with it. In terms of oil weight, an SAE 10 oil will vaporize more easily than an SAE 30 oil. This is another reason to switch to a higher viscosity if your car tends to use a bit of oil.

In the interest of better fuel economy and energy conservation, you may have switched from a straight SAE 30 or SAE 40 oil to a multigrade SAE 5W-20 for winter driving, which is a wise choice in cold climates. However, in the summer this lubricant may not be suitable for hot vacation driving and a higher-viscosity oil should be used, regardless of the slight loss in fuel economy. Remember the warning of API concerning lightweight SAE 5W and SAE 5W-20 grade oils: They "are not recommended for sustained high-speed driving." Be on the safe side—put a higher viscosity oil in the car for those long trips.

In the wintertime, regardless of what section of the country you live in, you should be using some type of "W"-(winter-) designated oil, 10W-30, for example. That "W" means it is meant for winter use—so use it. It has a special additive selection and is specifically formulated to protect against the ravages of winter driving conditions.

Multiviscosity oils such as SAE 10W-40 make use of modern chemistry and achieve their thick-thin capabilities through the addition of polymers. Engineers dub these oils "non-Newtonian" because they do the opposite of what physics says they should—they flow easily when cold and thicken when warm, offering the motorist maximum protection throughout a wide range of temperatures. However, these oils can "rupture" and lose much of their effective viscosity under certain conditions, such as sudden forceful accelerations. As mentioned earlier, sudden acceleration can squeeze oil from between bearing surfaces and the piston and cylinder wall. It can also cause permanent shear loss (oil breakdown) where the effective viscosity is diminished radically.

You should not use an oil of too low a viscosity under certain driving conditions. Just as 5W and 5W-20 oils should not be used for high-speed driving, they also should not be used under high temperature conditions, because their viscosity is inadequate to protect the engine under these circumstances. Continued use of thin oils can cause both excessive engine wear and increased oil consumption. This advice should also apply to single-grade 10W, 20, and 20W oils.

If "test data" comparisons show a number of oils with similar properties then a deciding factor should be whether the oil is designated as being "fuel efficient," "friction modified," "mileage-extending," "gas-saving" or "energy-conserving." "Energy-conserving" SG-rated oils are a notch above the regular SG oils because they can provide extra miles per tank of gas. To promote better mileage, some type of friction-fighting agent is incorporated into these "friction-modified" oils. These super-slippery oils (graphite and MoS2 oils fit this category) reduce engine friction. This not only means more miles per gallon but reduced engine wear to boot.

First-generation SF-rated oils with an "Energy Conserving" classification have, according to API, "produced a fuel economy improvement of 1.5 percent or greater over a standard reference oil in a standard test procedure." Of more interest are SG-rated oils that carry an "Energy Conserving II" designation. This new generation of friction-modified oils has produced a 2.7 percent increase (or greater) in fuel economy when compared to non–energy-conserving SG oils of the same viscosity. In its 1989 owner manuals, Ford Motor Company says "For maximum fuel economy benefits, use an oil with the Roman Numeral 'II' next to the words 'Energy Conserving' in the API Service Symbol." Not a bad idea no matter what kind of car you drive.

The lower portion of the donut-shaped API Service Symbol that appears on all oil containers is reserved for either the "Energy Conserving" or "Energy Conserving II" designations. If an oil has no energy-conserving properties, that area will be blank. (See Figure 13).

A while back I received this letter from a reader who was concerned that using higher weight multiviscosity oils might damage his engine:

> I was talking to some fellows recently, one of whom had attended a jamboree for motor-home owners in San Antonio, Texas. He said, and a couple of others agreed with him, that an authoritative person at one of the meetings claimed that multiviscosity oil would damage their engines.
>
> It seems that the chemicals added to 10W oil to make it 10W-40 would burn off or change at high temperatures and cause sludge to form in the engine and prevent proper lubrication, and that they would be better off using a single-viscosity oil.

I have learned from advertising, service-station operators and mechanics that just the opposite is true and that was the reason multiviscosity oil was invented. Am I fouling my engine by using 10W-40?

Do you really think that the major oil companies would make, and all major car companies recommend, multiviscosity oils if they were harmful to engines?

All this gibberish about multiviscosity oils' harming engines had its roots back in 1984, the year General Motors decided to abandon recommending higher-weight multiviscosity oils such as 10W-40 in favor of 5W-30 and 10W-30. GM mentioned studies (its own) showing that wide-range multiviscosity oils could cause engine deposits.

But GM achieved a 1.7 percent increase in its corporate average fuel economy by mandating use of lighter-weight 5W-30 and 10W-30 oils in its new cars.

And if 10W-40 could harm engines, don't you think 5W-30 could also, because it contains about the same amount of viscosity-extending polymers as 10W-40?

I've talked to engineers at major oil companies, and they all trace this unfortunate denigrating of 10W-40 and 20W-50 oils back to the GM action. All agree that no harm will befall any engine using these higher numbers.

Now, there is nothing wrong with single-grade oil, and many car, truck, and motor-home owners swear by it. But one of the main advantages multiviscosity has over single viscosity is that multiviscosity oil offers the engine a lot less resistance during the warm-up stage. This saves gasoline, engine work, and engine wear.

It is interesting to note that foreign-car manufacturers continue to recommend the higher-weight multiviscosity oils. But then again, most of them haven't had any problems meeting the fuel-economy standards imposed by Uncle Sam.

◊ ◊ ◊

Another reader wrote: "Several friends of mine believe that using diesel engine oil (either a CC or CD) in gasoline engines makes them last longer. They support this by saying that diesel oil works in harsher conditions—higher temperatures and on longer trips, as with long-haul semi-trailers—than oil for gasoline engines. Would it be better to use only a CC or CD diesel oil rather than one combined with a SG rating such as SG/CC?"

Logic would seem to indicate that the reader's friends are correct. Diesel oils have to deal with much higher engine temperatures, higher oxidation rates, sulfur deposits, fuel soot, acids and other deposits, and conditions not usually found in automobile gasoline engines. So it seems to make sense that using diesel oil in a gasoline engine would enhance its longevity.

But that isn't so. As we have seen, diesel oils are rated either API CC, CD, CDII, CE, or a combination such as CC/CD. If only these letters appear on the oilcan, it indicates that the oil is specifically formulated for diesel engines.

If you happen to be driving a new car, nowhere in the owner's manual will you see recommended a CC, CD, CDII, CE, or CC/CD, or other combination oil. All current gasoline engines require an API-rated SG oil. As we saw earlier, the SG can be in combination with CC, CD, or CE or even CC/CD (for example, SG-CC/CD), but you will never see just CC, CD, or CE recommended.

Why don't car manufacturers recommend CC-, CD-, or CE-rated oils for gasoline engines? It's because they fail in one critical area: API-rated CC, CD, CDII, or CE oils do not meet the engine-cleanliness parameters set by API for SG-rated gasoline engine oils.

As the reader mentioned, diesel engines are used under prolonged running conditions and higher temperatures, while gasoline engines normally see a lot of stop-and-go traffic. These different driving conditions, along with the differences between diesel fuel and gasoline, mean that different engine deposits must be controlled in each type of engine.

In a diesel engine the main deposits an oil must deal with are fuel soot and sulfur; in a gasoline engine the two main deposits are low-temperature sludge and varnish. What will keep a diesel engine clean fails to do the job in a gasoline engine because the deposits are different, the fuel is different, the running conditions are different, and the oil's additive package is different.

The above advice also applies to other specialty oils such as racing oils. At first glance it would seem that using an oil formulated for racing—readily available at most auto parts stores—would be a good thing. The logic goes something like this: If the oil is beneficial for a car operating under super severe service (racing), it must be extra good for my everyday car. However, just as in the example of diesel oils, that isn't the case.

Racing oils are formulated to protect against high-speed engine operation, extreme internal pressures, and high engine heat. They aren't designed for engines that are cold-started a lot or used for short trips, conditions that are very common in normal everyday driving. Racing oils won't protect as well against deposit formation in this kind of driving; they just aren't meant to do so. So leave the racing oils for the racers and hot rods and stick to an oil that will protect your engine during the type of driving you do most frequently.

Severe Service

If you are a typical driver you use your car mainly for trips of ten miles or less. You go to the store, drive to work, take the kids to school, go out for dinner on Saturday and every now and then take a Sunday drive. Once a year you may take that long drive to Grandma's at Christmas, or perhaps go on a summer vacation. Fairly normal driving, wouldn't you say? So you follow the recommendations in the car owner's manual and change oil in accordance with the "normal service" time or mileage intervals. What you don't realize, though, is that this type of "normal" driving isn't normal as far as the oil-change interval is concerned; this is really "severe service" driving. *Most* car owners use their cars the majority of the time under "severe service" conditions and not under so-called "normal" conditions. This is one of the main reasons automobile engines wear out so fast. The conscientious owner, thinking his driving is "normal," changes oil in accordance with the manufacturer's "normal" mileage or time recommendations, when in fact he should be following the recommendations for "severe service" driving. Let's see what qualifies as "severe service" and what is considered "normal."

All driving is not the same. Some types demand more from the engine and motor oil; other kinds of driving have very little effect on either and the car could literally run forever on the oil that is in it. A check of most owner's manuals will show that almost all list oil-change recommendations for what is considered "normal" operation and for "severe service" driving. Many fail to define exactly what is meant by "normal," or, as the American Petroleum Institute calls it, "ideal." The manuals do, however, define "severe service." The owner is then left with the feeling that anything that is not "severe service" must be "normal." This is very misleading, for in fact there are very few conditions of engine operation that could be classified as "normal" or "ideal."

API defines only one mode of engine operation as "ideal": when the car is moving at highway speeds on a paved road in a dustfree environment. Only under this condition should you follow the "normal" or maximum oil-change intervals given by the manufacturer. How many readers think their typical day-to-day driving will qualify as "ideal"? This point must be stressed: *Almost all driving done today is under "severe service" conditions of engine operation*, and oil-change recommendations for that type of driving should be followed. What, then, is "severe service"?

The American Petroleum Institute defines severe service as operations that include:

- Trips that are less than 10 miles (16.09 kilometers)
- Driving in dust or sand

- Cold weather that prevents full engine warm-up
- Idling for extended periods
- Stop-and-go driving
- Pulling trailers
- Heavy loads
- Operating in any other heavy-duty and severe service

"Operating in any other heavy-duty and severe service" means conditions such as sustained high-speed driving in hot weather and service that includes taxi, police, and ambulance-type driving. API goes on to say that

severe service operations represent the type of driving done by most motorists. One of the most frequent and severe types of driving is short trips with many stops and starts. Under such conditions, engines do not reach normal operating temperatures, particularly in cold weather. For his protection the *MOTORIST SHOULD RECOGNIZE THESE SEVERE SERVICE OPERATIONS AND FOLLOW THE RECOMMENDATIONS OF THE CAR MANUFACTURERS.*

Two points should be emphasized again. One of the most *frequent and severe* types of driving is *short trips with many stops and starts.* Isn't this *your* most frequent type of driving? The other thing is that *the motorist should recognize these severe service operations.* If you don't know what severe service is, how can you protect against its ravages? This is one of the major flaws of most owner's manuals—there is very little emphasis, if any at all, placed on the fact that almost all driving done today is severe and the motorist should take the necessary steps to combat the damage it can do. Oil-change recommendations should be printed in big red letters and the car owner made aware of the *real* facts about oil-change frequency. In fact, for all practical purposes the maximum or "normal" oil-change recommendations should be done away with altogether, as too many owners are lulled into thinking that their driving is just like their neighbors' and just about like everyone else's, so it must be "normal."

Since the original edition of *Drive It Forever* was published in 1983, many automobile manufacturers have returned to recommending shorter interval oil changes and have also defined what normal and severe service driving is. These were problems in earlier owner's manuals, which led many owners to mistakenly believe that changing oil according to the normal oil-change recommendations was best for their cars. I like to think that *Drive It Forever* had some influence in prodding the manufacturers to redo and redefine oil change procedures.

The Oil Change—New Blood for the Engine

It would be nice if all cars had some type of electronic oil sensor that would activate a dash light whenever some additive in the oil became depleted or the contaminants in the oil reached a point where they could be harmful. This "time to change oil" light would be a boon to motorists everywhere and would solve one of the stickiest problems that has faced car owners since the first car rolled off the assembly line: How long should the oil be kept in the engine? Unfortunately, cars are not equipped with such a device (although with our present technology they probably could be), and the owner must decide when to change the oil. Ideally, the oil should be changed before any one of its additives becomes depleted and is no longer effective, but not before its total useful life is up. The problem is, how can you tell when one of these additives is beginning to lose effectiveness? If we all were chemists and had labs in our garages, it wouldn't be a problem, but we aren't, and it is. Let's look closely at this dilemma and see if we can find an answer to the most crucial question a car owner can ask: When should I change my oil?

Oil Contamination

The clue to the answer to the question of *when* should we change the oil lies in another question: *Why* do we change our oil? We change because of the:

- Accumulation of contaminants in the oil, and
- Chemical changes (additive depletion and oxidation) in the makeup of the oil itself.

These two factors cause deterioration of the oil and prevent it from doing an efficient job of lubricating and cooling engine parts.

As a car is driven, the level of contaminants in the motor oil is constantly increasing. Since combustion products are continually being formed and picked up by the oil, it becomes more and more difficult for the oil to protect and lubricate the engine.

As an example, the additives which disperse sludge-forming materials and prevent rust and corrosion are used up in performing their function, much as a cake of soap is used up as it does its job. When this additive depletion reaches a certain point, the oil can no longer do its job and must be changed.

The rate at which contamination and additive depletion occur depends on a number of variables. One of these is driving habits, which vary greatly and have a direct effect on the useful life of the oil. Other factors include the precision of ignition and carburetion adjustments, air cleaner service, and the mechanical condition of the engine. The latter is often reflected in the amount of blowby to the crankcase, which increases as the wear condition of the engine deteriorates. It is a significant contributor to oil contamination. Blowby is a condition of a usually worn engine in which combustion gases escape past the piston rings (which normally would prevent this) into the upper cylinder and manifold area of the engine.

A neglected PCV system can cause rapid oil deterioration and deposit buildup. Higher under-hood temperatures, brought about by the use of power accessories, required exhaust emission equipment and basic engine adjustments also contribute to oil deterioration. This deterioration will also increase if oil filters are not replaced regularly. But even a clean, high-quality filter, while it is effective in removing abrasives from the oil, cannot filter out fuel dilution and other sources of liquid contamination. All of these factors affect the rate at which motor oil becomes contaminated and its additives are depleted.

The reader should be aware that the oil itself does not "wear out"; it is the additive package incorporated in the oil that becomes depleted. The best insurance of sufficient additive content is a frequent change of fresh oil. New oil, combined with a new filter, at precisely prescribed intervals, will do more to promote engine longevity and performance than any other single thing the car owner can do.

So When Should I Change It?

According to the American Petroleum Institute, motor oil should be changed at "regular intervals" with close attention being paid to the car manufacturer's "severe service" oil-change recommendation. Now we're getting somewhere. Let's narrow this down even more so you will have no doubt about when you should drain the oil.

Rule Number One: Ignore the "normal" or maximum oil-drain intervals given in the car owner's operating manual.

Rule Number Two: See what the manual's "severe service" recommendations are. There will be two recommendations given here, one for time and one for mileage; for instance, change oil every 3 months or 3,000 miles, whichever comes first. Using these severe service intervals as a guide, we come to . . .

Rule Number Three: Cut the severe service recommendations by 10 percent in the summer and by 20 percent in the winter. Using the above interval of 3 months or 3,000 miles as an example, we would be changing at 2,700 miles in the summer and 2,400 miles in the winter. If the time interval elapses before the mileage is accumulated (chances are good that it will), we then change at about 80 days in the summer and 70 days in the winter. These should be your *maximum* oil-change intervals. To repeat: If the owner's manual says to change every 3 months or 3,000 miles, whichever comes first, for severe service driving, this translates to 2,700 miles or 80 days, whichever comes first (summer), and 2,400 miles or 70 days, whichever comes first (winter).

The foregoing schedule will provide the motorist with maximum protection and will virtually ensure that you won't be driving with contaminated or additive-depleted oil. Granted, it may cost you a few dollars more because of the more frequent oil changes, but in the long run it will return those dollars many times over.

These recommendations should always be tempered with a stiff dose of common sense. If you are taking a cross-country trip in the summer and will be putting 7,000 miles on the car, it would be a waste of oil to change it at 2,700 miles because the car will be used under the most ideal conditions: paved road driving at highway speeds in a dustfree (we hope) environment. In this case you can say you are the exception and are actually driving under those "ideal" conditions; oil-drain intervals can be lengthened considerably. Or perhaps you become caught in a bad dust storm or must, because of your job, drive over dirt roads for a number of months at a time. Logic tells you that this is severe service driving and you should shorten your oil-drain interval accordingly.

This brings us to another type of driving—one you won't find in the operator's manual but one each and every owner should be aware of. It is our own special category of "Super Severe Service."

◇ ◇ ◇

What is "Super Severe Service"? This is any type of driving that qualifies as "Severe Service" but that, because of adverse climatic conditions, is made even more severe, and calls for an even more shortened oil-change interval. If you are caught in a severe dust storm and must drive through it for one reason or another, this is "super severe service" and the special conditions dictate that you change oil at the first possible chance, regardless of the time left to your scheduled change interval. Towing a trailer is severe service; towing a trailer in mountainous country in very hot weather is super severe service, and in this case the owner should note the number of miles driven under this service and count them at least *double* when changing oil. So if you drove 500 miles through the mountains with a trailer, figure it as 1,000 miles when considering the next oil change. The main point is that the motorist must be aware that special oil- and filter-change precautions should be taken whenever common sense tells you you have called on your car's engine for super severe service. Luckily for the average motorist, that won't be very often.

Figure 15 shows how rapidly (the curve dips down steeply after the "dump-out" point) motor oil loses its ability to hold debris in suspension when it is kept in the vehicle too long. We always want to change oil somewhere near the top of the curve, but never wait until after the "dump-out" point has been reached. By following the preceding oil change recommendations, you will be changing on the upside of the curve, before any contaminants can be deposited or wear-fighting additives lose effectiveness.

The engine should always be at or near operating temperature before you change the oil. Hot oil flows better than cold oil, so you won't leave half a quart of dirty cold oil and sludge inside the engine. Hot oil also indicates the engine was used recently; that means the contaminants are more likely to be in suspension, where they can be drained off easily. As the oil cools, some of the solids settle out and are not removed by the drainout.

Take your time and let *all* the oil drain from the crankcase. This is

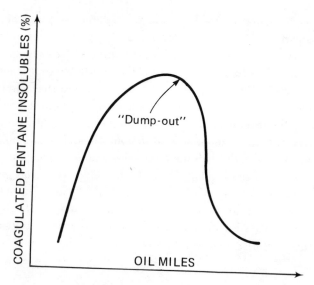

Figure 15. Oil performance in relation to oil-change life.

easy if you change oil yourself, but a station attendant may be in a hurry and may replace the drain plug before all the oil is out. Ask that *all* the oil be allowed to exit. The drain plug should be wiped clean before it is replaced. If you have a magnetic drain plug, wipe off all metal shavings prior to replacing the plug.

◇ ◇ ◇

"Contains Petroleum Distillates." Those three words on an engine cleaner-additive shouldn't be taken lightly. Engine purges, or "enemas," as I prefer to call them, contain powerful chemicals (petroleum distillates) that can clean gum, varnish, sludge, and even carbon from an engine's insides.

If you use one of these cleaners—street wisdom says to use them just prior to an oil change to "get all the junk out"—be aware that they can dislodge "false seals" in older higher mileage engines. These "seals" (usually some type of postcombustion product buildup) often prevent oil from entering the combustion chamber and burning off. In fact, one major car manufacturer has recently claimed that, in some cases, these deposits or false seals help the engine run better.

In older cars engine cleaners can dislodge the false seals, causing the car to use oil, sometimes excessively. Think twice before using any type of cleaner in your older engine. And a newer car's engine shouldn't need one: Frequent oil changes with a high-quality oil are all that is necessary to keep its insides sparkling clean and deposit-free. If the oil additive's label reads *"Contains Petroleum Distillates,"* put it back.

When choosing between the time and mileage oil-change intervals, recall that the time is usually reached before the mileage is. If you want to pick just one interval and stick with it, time is usually the best bet.

But don't forget the "whichever comes first" rule previously discussed. If the time interval, for instance, three months, is up before the mileage interval, you should still change the oil regardless of the number of miles since the last oil change. As we have seen, oil can lose its protective qualities even when the car is not being used. Changing on a "whichever comes first" schedule allows for maximum engine protection.

Keep accurate records—from gas mileage to oil change to weather conditions. Always note the mileage and date of your last oil change. Keep track of the type of driving done and, in general, the type of weather during this interval. This will help in deciding on whether you might safely lengthen the time between changes or if you should shorten it. Weather and type of driving are two major factors in determining when it is time to get rid of the old oil and put in the new. If there is ever any doubt about extending or shortening the oil-change interval, follow this advice: "When in doubt, change it."

If you are going to be pulling a trailer or another car for any distance, the best precaution you can take is to have the oil and filter changed just prior to starting the tow. This will prevent oil "breakdown" during the tow. Long-range trailer towing—or any kind of towing for that matter—is one of the most severe of all engine and transmission tasks. Fresh oil is excellent insurance that you will get where you are going with minimal wear on the vehicle.

As an engine wears, the oil is more likely to become contaminated because of the increased blowby. This means that on older engines, even closer attention should be paid to the oil change to slow down the wear process. In older engines it is also important to keep the oil level near the full mark. This will help prevent the engine from burning more oil.

◇ ◇ ◇

Putting off an oil change or a lube job for whatever reason is false economy. Don't procrastinate and don't be lazy when it comes to the periodic servicing of your car. The oil doesn't have to be changed *that* often. Be sure to do required services within the time or mileage framework of your individualized schedule.

Many larger cities have analytical labs that offer a service called "oil analysis." By sampling a part of oil taken at oil-change time, the lab can determine how much wear-producing metal is present, how diluted the oil is either with fuel or water, what its present viscosity is, and a host of other properties. This can be a valuable tool for an occasional check of your oil because it can help determine if your oil-change interval is correct. Dirty, additive-depleted, polluted, highly viscous oil means your oil-change interval is too long and should be shortened accordingly; oil with little or no viscosity change and minor abrasive content means you are on the right track as far as your change interval is concerned, and you may, if the test results so indicate, even safely extend the drain interval a bit. This service, where available, usually costs about ten dollars, and is well worth the occasional cash outlay.

Precautions to Take When Changing Oil

If you choose to change the oil yourself, there are a number of precautions you should take with both yourself and the old oil. Pennzoil advises always using good personal hygiene practices when changing oil. These include:

- Avoiding prolonged skin contact with old or new oil.
- Washing thoroughly with soap and water.
- Using waterless hand cleaners to help clean hands.
- Never using gasoline, thinners, or solvents to clean hands.
- Avoiding skin contact with oil-soiled clothing.
- Laundering soiled clothing before wearing again.
- Discarding oil-soaked shoes or other unwashable articles of clothing.

Then there's the old oil itself. Every precaution should be taken in disposing of it. Just because the oil you just drained out of the engine originally came from the ground, that doesn't mean that it should be put back there. Used oil isn't the same as the benign crude that came from down deep—it contains many harmful contaminants and chemicals. Don't pour old oil onto the ground or throw it in the trash or dump it in ditches or sewers. It can be carried off by rains and pollute streams and underground water aquifers.

Never mix the old oil with other substances such as solvents. Store the old oil in non-leaking containers and save it for recycling by a reputable collector or used-oil processor. Many cities have waste-oil collection and disposal centers. Check your yellow pages or call the city or state health departments for locations near you.

Oil Filters

Many car manufacturers recommend that the oil filter be changed at every other oil change. We think this is pure folly. Change the oil filter each and every time the oil is changed. The filter contains approximately one quart of dirty, contaminated, additive-depleted oil. Why put this back into circulation with the fresh oil? It doesn't make good sense. On many smaller engines with a small oil crankcase capacity of three or four quarts, leaving the filter in would mean leaving a quarter to a third of the crankcase contaminated with old oil. This means that the new oil would lose a full quarter to a third of its effectiveness; it would instantly have to use up much of its additive content just to fight the old oil left in the filter. Don't skimp on this very important part of the oil change. Always change the filter with the oil for maximum protection.

Most modern engines use what is called a full-flow filtering system. This means that, under normal conditions with a clean filter and clean oil, the entire output of the oil pump passes through the oil filter before going into circulation in the engine.

Theoretically, a full-flow filter cleans all the oil all the time. This is not always true in practice, however. Oil thickens in cold weather and may not flow readily through the filtering material. And, like oil itself, oil filters gradually become contaminated and lose their effectiveness. For these reasons, a filter bypass valve is incorporated in the filter or in the filtering system. If the filter becomes clogged, the valve opens and the pump output goes directly into circulation in the engine. This system will prevent immediate engine failure, but it should be remembered that the oil lubricating the engine under these conditions is unfiltered oil carrying abrasive particles and other harmful contaminants.

It should also be pointed out that even the best full-flow oil filter, while effective in removing abrasives, will not filter out liquid materials such as water, unburned fuel, or acids. Filters do not remove dilution nor prevent rust and corrosive wear. (emphasis mine)

Today's quality oil filters, in the main, trap contaminant particles approximately 15 microns and larger in size. The smaller particles slip through the net. Cheaper, bargain-brand oil filters may not trap even larger particles or, if they do, don't have the capacity to trap many and go into the bypass stage much quicker than do high-grade filters. With oil filters, you get what you pay for—most of the time.

Filters can and do become clogged and lose their effectiveness. Does it make sense then to leave in an admittedly partially clogged filter when changing the oil? The filter could become completely clogged halfway to the next oil change and for that entire period, the engine would be paying the price of having contaminants, especially abrasives, taking license with it. As the man in the TV ad says, we can pay him now or we can pay him later. Let's pay him now—it's a lot cheaper in the long run.

There is another reason why it is important the filter be changed along with the oil, especially in cold weather. The contaminated oil in the filter has a higher viscosity because of the particulate matter held in it. This will raise the entire viscosity of the new oil at a time (winter) when the lower viscosity of the fresh oil is desirable.

If for some reason you are stuck in a place that doesn't have your kind of filter, then it is far better to change the oil and leave the old filter in than not change the oil at all.

Many car owners fight the initial wear caused by the dry start immediately after the oil and filter have been changed by priming the new oil filter. That is, they fill the filter with fresh oil before installing it. Although this does allow for quicker oil circulation—the filter doesn't have to be filled first—some manufacturers advise against the practice. Check your owner's manual before entertaining any idea of priming your filter.

At any rate, the amount of wear caused by that second or so of dry running immediately after an oil and filter change is insignificant. Remember, anti-wear agents from the previous oil are bonded to the cylinder walls and surfaces where metal-to-metal contact is probable. They should be able to protect sufficiently for that second or two. In addition, if you use a moly-type additive in the oil, the moly will be chemically attached to the metal surfaces and no metal-to-metal contact will occur.

When allowed, priming the oil filter won't do any harm, but the benefits, for the most part, have been greatly exaggerated.

Oil Additives—Add Your Own for Longer Engine Life

When one object slides over another, a resistance is set up in the form of friction between the objects. The engine has lots of parts trying to slide over one another and consequently produces a lot of friction. This is combatted by placing something between the objects—namely, oil. Oil reduces the friction, cuts down on the heat produced by the friction, and prevents wear or seizure that could be caused by the friction. The higher the lubricity or slipperiness of the oil, the less friction and wear it will allow. Engineers measure a lubricant's ability to resist friction by a number known as the coefficient of friction. This number or value can range anywhere from 0 to 1.0—the higher the number, the poorer the lubrication qualities. Straight mineral oil (essentially motor oil that has nothing added) has a value of around .15 to .22. Graphite, a commonly used oil additive, is about .07 to .15. Molybdenum disulfide (moly) is .025 to .10.

Adding graphite or moly to the oil can significantly enhance its lubricating qualities because it will effectively lower the overall coefficient of friction of the oil. In 1978 in *How to Get More Miles per Gallon*, I reported that

recent tests conducted independently by the Ethyl Corporation, Automotive Research Associates, and Loughborough Consultants

Limited have shown that a 2–12 percent improvement in gas mileage can be expected if molybdenum disulfide (MoS2) is added to the crankcase oil. "Moly" oil additives have been around for years, but the recent gas shortage has brought their remarkable lubricating qualities to the public eye. MoS2 additives are now available at many auto parts stores under various commercial names. Molybdenum disulfide, when combined with regular motor oil, dramatically enhances its lubricating qualities and cuts internal engine friction, a major cause of gasoline consumption. "Moly" will also tangentially reduce fuel consumption due to its effect on increased cranking (starting) speed at low temperatures. The reduction in friction is beneficial during the entire "warm-up" period, when fuel demands are highest.

Using figures from a U.S. Department of Transportation study, we see that a driver averaging 12,000 miles per year while getting an average of 12 mpg (a bit low for today) with gas at $1.25 per gallon can save about $58 a year on gasoline alone when MoS2 is added to the oil. The additional savings in reduced engine wear can't be quantitatively measured but are significant.

Since the above was written, a number of commercially available oils with either MoS2 or graphite (a similar substance) in them have appeared. The extra protection provided by these solid lubricants can be valuable. In fact, many engineers recommend the addition of some type of "lamellar solid lubricant" to the motor oil to help prevent corrosion and ensure maximum lubrication and protection in upper-cylinder engine areas. Don't let the words "lamellar solid lubricant" scare you—that's just a fancy name for our old reliable friends MoS2 and graphite.

There are times during engine operation when lubrication to certain areas (boundary areas) is minimal and metal-to-metal contact is greatly increased. One time is during the cold start; another is while the engine is running under high load. Keeping the surfaces separated, even though little or no oil may be available, is still possible by using either a graphite or MoS2 additive in the oil.

All other conditions being equal, oils containing graphite or MoS2 as part of their additive package should be considered superior to oils without them. The car owner also has the option of adding commercially available preparations of MoS2 to the present oil. One of the big consumer drawbacks to graphite or MoS2 oil preparations is the black appearance they give to the motor oil, which is not appealing to many motorists. Appearances can be deceiving, and in this case should be ignored completely; these additives do work and can be valuable aids in the fight against engine deterioration.

◇ ◇ ◇

Recently a new class of lubricants has come on the automotive market. Teflon-type engine additives claim to be a one-time permanent treatment that bonds Teflon or similar particles to the moving and stationary engine parts, thereby reducing friction. There may be something to these claims. Teflon, Halon, and Fluon are trade names for a class of chemicals called PTFE or TFE, polytetrafluoroethylene or tetrafluoroethylene, if you will. These products have a coefficient of friction of about .04 on the average, considerably less than graphite or MoS2. Most preparations are in liquid form and are rather expensive. If they can live up to their claims of reduced engine wear and more miles per gallon, they will be well worth the money invested in them. They won't do your engine any harm if used according to instructions. There is also a powdered fluorocarbon additive available that claims the same results and is substantially less expensive. If you choose to use one of these engine additives, do not use it with an oil that already contains graphite or MoS2. I would not use any powdered fluorocarbons, however, as there is too much present evidence that they can agglomerate and plug engine oil passages.

At least one major manufacturer and distributor of PTFE lubricants is currently testing a colloidally suspended PTFE formulation. In the past, a number of noncolloidally suspended products contributed to engine sludge buildup because the PTFE particles tended to settle out. Suspending PTFE molecules colloidally should insure that these super slippery particles are dispersed throughout the oil at all times where they can do the most good.

"Shake Well Before Using." Paying attention to those four words could save your engine a lot of grief. How's that? When considering any type of oil additive, read the label carefully. If the warning *"Shake Well Before Using"* appears on the label, steer clear of that product.

Why be concerned about this? If you need to shake the can first, the product isn't suspended and its active ingredients have probably settled to the bottom of the container. The product will also settle in your engine where it will add to sludge buildup. Some oil additives are properly suspended, but many—too many—aren't. Be certain any engine oil additive you are considering is one you don't have to shake, rattle, and roll before using.

Miscellaneous

Don't wait until the oil is a quart low before adding. There is no law saying you can't add half a quart and put the other half away. A full crankcase guarantees the engine will have the maximum amount of oil available to it at all times. Each time you add even a small amount of fresh oil, you are recharging the entire lubricating system with fresh additives. This practice can be even more beneficial in small-crankcase-capacity engines. If the engine only holds about three quarts of oil and you wait until it is a quart low before adding, the engine operates that entire period with as little as two-thirds of the oil that could be available to it. It may be a bit more inconvenient to add oil this way, but the benefits will more than offset the inconvenience.

Another reason for keeping the oil "full" and never—but *never*—allowing it to get below the "add" mark is that about 40 percent of the engine is directly dependent upon the oil to cool it. Oil must act as a coolant for such vital parts as the bearings, crankshaft, and timing gears; in fact most of the lower engine depends upon a constant supply of circulating oil to cool it. The more oil in the crankcase, the better its ability to remove heat. In a small engine, the cooling capacity is increased by 33 percent and in a large one by about 20 percent by keeping the oil above the add mark. This point becomes more critical when hot outside temperatures demand additional cooling from the oil. Oil is a vital cooling fluid—keep it topped off for maximum engine protection.

◇ ◇ ◇

One of the reasons cars don't last as long as we would like them to is that too little emphasis is placed on the importance of the oil, and the oil and filter change. A check of a number of books on car maintenance shows that the oil change and type of oil selected are treated as just another service to be performed. Many of these books advocate (as do many new car manuals) changing the filter at every other oil change. This is like operating on a man who has five bullets in him and only removing four, reasoning that the next bullet can be taken out during his next operation. Don't skimp on oil, oil filters, or oil changes.

◇ ◇ ◇

Don't be disturbed if the high-quality SG oil you purchased turns dark soon after you put it in the engine. There is nothing wrong with the oil, it's just doing its job. Turning dark is an indication that the detergents and dispersants are working to clean out and hold in suspension the contaminant particles that would otherwise collect and form sludge. This is one of the important functions of a good detergent/dispersant oil.

◇ ◇ ◇

As previously recommended, owners of small four-cylinder cars should use an SG-rated oil to get the extra anti-wear and anti-scuff properties.

These engines work a lot harder than a lazy V-8 and need all the protection they can get. Oil-change periods should also be followed very closely.

Turbo-charged engines fall automatically under the heading of severe service when it comes to the oil change. Check manufacturer's suggestions for turbo-charged cars and then use our "super severe service" recommendations to get the proper oil-change interval. These engines run hotter and the oil is subject to oxidation and deterioration. Turbo-charger bearings run under high loads and very close tolerances, demanding more from the oil. To protect against premature failure, the oil should be changed more frequently.

With the increasing popularity of turbo-charged engines, oil manufacturers have come up with a new class of oils specifically formulated for use in turbos. These "turbo oils" have customized additive packages that resist the high heat generated in the turbo itself (the turbo also depends on engine oil for lubrication) and the engine. The main extra ingredient is an anti-oxidation additive that helps resist oil breakdown under high-heat conditions.

What happens if you mix two different weights of oil, such as a 10W-20 and a 10W-40? Will the result be a mix of the two or will it be a separate, homogeneous oil? Because a lot of car owners at one time or another mix oils, let's see what happens when you do it.

If you mix different weights of oil, whether single weight or multigrade, the resultant mixture will have a single weight or viscosity designation. If you mix equal amounts of SAE 20 and SAE 40, you end up with SAE 30. If you mix equal amounts of multigrades, you end up with a single multigrade. Two quarts of SAE 10W-20 and two quarts of SAE 10W-40 will produce four quarts of SAE 10W-30.

The molecules of each oil are not affected when the oils are mixed. They join to form another oil with different viscosity. Just as adding more water to a heavy dough mixture will make it thinner, adding a thinner, lower-viscosity oil to a heavier, higher-viscosity oil will thin the resulting homogeneous mix.

What about the extended-drain synthetic oils that promise anywhere from 15,000 to 25,000 miles (and higher) between oil changes? Can they be used profitably? First of all, let's remember that the oil-change interval promised by these oils is for "normal" or "ideal" driving conditions. As we have seen, this type of driving is very rare, and for all practical purposes any change intervals based on "normal" driving can be ignored. If these extended-drain interval figures were translated into severe service terms, the mileage figures would drop considerably: The 15,000-mile oil would need to be changed every 6,000 miles, and the 25,000-mile oil would be reduced to 10,000 miles. These figures make the oils sound more realistic but are still rather high. If you choose to use synthetic oil in your car, be aware that most manufacturers' warranty requirements do not make exceptions for synthetic oils. You can use them, but they still must be changed in accordance with the warranty requirements, which usually are based on regular mineral oil.

Synthetics are special oils made with some type of man-made base fluid, usually an ester or similar compound. Conventional motor oils, on the other hand, are made from a mineral-oil base stock.

Synthetics have been around for a number of years now and many of the bugs have been taken out of them. They are a highly reliable class of lubricating fluids. They are expensive—one quart costs approximately the same as three or four quarts of high-quality mineral oil. They can give better service than conventional mineral oils over the same period of use, the only point of contention being "how long can they safely be used?" This controversy is still to be resolved. To be on the safe side, leave synthetics in the crankcase double the amount of time you would have left your regular oil in; in no cases should this time exceed triple the period of your regular change interval.

A couple of cautions are in order concerning synthetic oils. If the engine has a lot of miles or has been mistreated, switching from a mineral oil to a synthetic could cause it to use more oil. Synthetics are sometimes higher in detergent additive content, and this can have the same effect as petroleum distillate engine purges: It can loosen lodged deposits—sure, you now have a cleaner engine, but it may now use more oil. Used in a solid low-mileage engine, they pose no problem.

I personally would not use synthetic oil in a new car until it had logged about 5,000 miles. Its super-slippery nature could interfere with the proper breaking in of the engine. Parts may not get the opportunity to wear in, mate properly, and find their best working surfaces. After 5,000 miles, no problem.

One final suggestion: If you live in an area where frequent oil changes may be required (because of dust storms, sandy or dirt roads, extremely cold or wet weather) it may not be worth your while to use synthetics because you should be changing oil more frequently. The price of synthetics may not warrant their use in this case.

For those of you who have adopted a wait-and-see attitude concerning synthetic or extended-drain oils, much of the benefit of a full change of synthetic can be obtained by adding only one quart of synthetic to the regular oil at the next change. If your car holds five quarts, add four quarts of your usual oil and one quart of synthetic. Make certain that both oils have the same API service designation (never mix service designations) and they will be fully compatible. By adding just one quart of synthetic, you spread many of its special qualities throughout all the oil. This is an excellent way to test synthetics in your car without having to pay the price of a full change.

Since the original edition of this book was published six years ago, a new service-oriented phenomenon has popped up in the automotive aftermarket: 10-minute lube and oil-change facilities. These "quick lubes" are a boon to the car owner who either doesn't know how or doesn't have time to do his own car servicing. I've had personal experience with a number of them—most notably Chicago's Oil Express chain—and for the most part find them excellent places to have a car lubed and its oil changed. With quick lubes popping up in every town like mushrooms after a rain, car owners have no excuse for driving around with old, additive-depleted oil in the crankcase. There should be more *Drive It Forever* cars around now that quick lubes are part of the aftermarket.

5

The Cold Start—A Time of Accelerated Engine Wear

The most important and critical time for an engine is that period from when the car is *cold-started* to when it is fully warmed. It is during this time that much wear occurs and fuel consumption is the highest. This is the engine's time of least efficiency; in fact, an engine during this cold period may use as little as 3 percent of the energy available in a gallon of gasoline—the rest is wasted. On the other hand, this is one of the times when the diligent owner can make great inroads in his or her battle to make the engine last longer, for anything done to combat this cold-engine wear and inefficiency will pay multiple dividends. With this in mind, let's look now at ways that will prove invaluable in the quest for more miles per car.

The Cold Start

Once you have started a cold engine and the oil pressure gauge or light indicates normal, place the car gently in gear and get moving. No more than fifteen seconds of engine idling should be required. *Do not* try to warm the engine by prolonged idling. Years ago this was the accepted practice, but with today's engines and increased knowledge of the mechanics of engine wear and fuel economy, most engineers are in agreement that prolonged idling of a cold engine will only do harm. A cold-idling engine won't warm as fast, lubricate as efficiently, or burn gasoline as completely as one that is in gear and moving—that is, one that is under load. Get that car moving as soon as possible because this hastens the warm-up, allows the automatic choke to step down to a less rich mixture much faster, and permits the oil to circulate better, lubricating vital points at the exact time when they most need it. Use slow to moderate speeds the first few miles and don't race or gun the engine.

A cursory check of a number of new-car owner's manuals will show that most manufacturers are in agreement with the above, recommending that cold-engine-idle warm-up periods be short.

Let's go through the whole cold-start procedure again in a bit more detail as it is one of the very most important techniques to be mastered in the quest for a long-lasting car.

Press the accelerator pedal completely to the floor and let it return. Then press it down about two-thirds of the way and hold it there; wait a second or two and then turn the key. A properly tuned engine should fire up immediately. Due to variations in engine design, some engines may need an extra pump or two of the accelerator to start up. If you have an owner's manual, check its recommendations. After a few cold starts you should be able to determine exactly the amount of accelerator feed needed to fire the engine. (Note: Most fuel-injected engines do not require that the accelerator be depressed before or during a cold or warm start. Check your owner's manual for the proper cold-start procedure.)

Once the engine is running, wait a few seconds to be certain proper oil pressure has been established. The oil pressure light should be out or the gauge should read normal. Check the owner's manual again to determine what is "normal" for your make and model car. Some cars may take longer to reach "normal" pressure than others, but in most cases the total cold-idling period immediately following the engine start should not be more than fifteen seconds. Forget about what dad or grandad told you about warming up the engine—you are dealing with a new breed of engines, fuels, and oils.

Once oil pressure has been established, place the car gently in gear and start moving. Use slow, judicious speeds for the first few miles, remembering never to gun or race the motor. Gradually—repeat: *gradually*—build up to your desired speed. If traffic conditions are such that they do not allow you to gradually build speed, then go with the minimum speed practical for conditions encountered.

Keep in mind that on a day with an outside temperature of 78°F (a nice warm day, right?) it still takes about ten to fifteen minutes for a car to become warmed to the point of maximum efficiency. On a very cold day the car may never reach total efficiency, as parts such as transmission, wheel bearings, axles, and tires never have a chance to become fully warmed. By following every tip given in this book on engine warm-up you assure yourself that you are doing everything possible to get the best performance with minimal wear under the most adverse of conditions—the cold start.

Not nearly enough emphasis has been placed on the precautions that must be observed during a cold start or during short trips with a cold engine. When the car is fully warmed and on the open highway, you can almost forget about wear—it is virtually nonexistent. But, as we have seen, the greatest portion of mechanical wear in an engine occurs during the cold start and on short trips where the auto never has a chance to reach normal operating temperature. These are the areas where you, the car owner, should take every action to allay their destructive tendencies.

This cold-start recommendation should, of course, be tempered with the advice in your owner's manual. Many small-car manufacturers recommend up to five pumps of the accelerator before cold-starting the engine. This may be the case with your car and more priming of the engine may be necessary. Experiment with different numbers of pumps and choose the one that proves most effective for you. In most cases, one complete depression followed by holding the pedal half to two-thirds of the way down while turning the key will do the trick.

One of the complaints I get at seminars and speeches and in letters to my column is from drivers who try to use the minimum cold-idling technique but fail because their cars won't run without stalling until they have warmed up for a few minutes. If a car is tuned properly, there shouldn't be any problem starting out after 15 seconds or so of cold-engine idling. Most of the time balky cold-engine performance can be traced to an ignition or fuel system that isn't working properly. A tuned car is a prerequisite before accomplishing minimum idling starts.

In the event you have a car that still refuses to run when cold, even if it's properly tuned, idle it the minimum amount of time needed to operate without stalling.

Run without your car's heater until the vehicle is fully warmed. Heaters use up a lot of the engine's heat, which could be used to warm the engine to operating temperature more rapidly. Keep heaters off until the engine reaches normal or near normal operating temperature. Anyway, if the engine isn't warm the heater doesn't work too well, and no heat is better than cool moving air.

When starting a cold engine (or an engine that is warm, for that matter) it is desirable that it fire up on the first turn of the key. Continual grinding of a cold engine, accompanied by the diluting effect of raw gas being frantically pumped into the cylinders, won't do the engine any good. There are four main actors on stage when your engine is cranked over and each plays a vital role in ensuring that cranking speed is sufficient to get the car started. These four items are the battery, the battery cables, the starter motor, and the engine oil. We take for granted here that the engine is in proper tune and all is in order. Why is engine oil included in these four? It plays a major role in cold-starting because the oil puts up a natural resistance to moving parts; the more resistance, the harder it is for the engine to be started. Besides having the battery, battery cables, and starter motor in top condition, the selection of an oil that will remain fluid and moves easily when cold is of prime importance during the cold-start operation.

Keep your car garaged or under a carport. If this isn't possible, then any type of shelter over or around the car will help. Trees, a wall, the side of a house—all provide some protection from the elements. In cold, windy climates shelter is a must, because moving air can greatly hasten the rate at which an engine cools. Shelter from the wind and cold will do more to promote good winter gas mileage than any other single item. Remember, it took gasoline to warm the engine, and anything you can do to conserve the heat will improve mileage.

In hot, dry, or dusty climates a garaged car is impervious to gasoline evaporation. As much as a quart can be lost on extremely hot, windy days if the car is left outside. Garaging your car also eliminates the problem of dust entering the engine compartment where it can clog the carburetor and air cleaner. In wet climates, shelter guards against the frustrations of a wet ignition.

Although a sheltered car will give better mileage, it will, perhaps more importantly, give more miles, too. A garaged car will just last longer than one left outside at the mercy of the elements. Sheltering the car gives you a great advantage in the quest for extended engine and total car life. It is one of the most important things any owner can do for his or her car. Unfortunately, many of us do not have the luxury of a garage or a carport. If this is your case your battle will be tougher, but remember that any shelter you find for your vehicle is better than none. And if you do have a carport or garage, don't be guilty of the cardinal sin of being too lazy to pull the car in. Those few seconds you spend putting the car away could literally mean years of extra life from your vehicle.

Question: At what temperature will an engine run most efficiently and last the longest? Answer: At the thermostat temperature given by the manufacturer for that particular type of engine. This is the temperature at which your particular vehicle was designed to function most efficiently and is the temperature we talk about when we say a car has reached normal operating temperature (NOT) or is fully warmed. NOT = maximum efficiency = less engine work = less wear.

Pay very close attention to this next suggestion, for it is one of the most important ones in this book. If yours is a two-or-more-car family and you must use a car to make a short trip (one of five miles or less), *always* take the car that has been used last. The reason should be obvious: That's the car with the warmest engine. Why take the car that hasn't been started all day and run it a few miles under the most severe of conditions—a short trip with a cold engine? Using the car that is already warm means you don't have to go through the cold-start and accelerated wear syndrome *again*—the warm car has already paid its dues and any wear occurring during the short trip will be minimal compared to what the cold car would experience. Other tangential benefits of using the warm car are that on a cold day the heater will work better and the warm car will give more miles per gallon. So always use the warm car when you have a choice. By practicing this car-saving technique you extend the effective life of *both* cars, not just one. It's a simple practice but put it to work for you and watch the lives of both of your cars start to stretch out.

Under normal warmed-up driving conditions, most cars achieve maximum engine efficiency with a carburetor air/fuel ratio of about 15 parts air to 1 part fuel (15 : 1). During a cold start it is not unusual to find this ratio reduced to around 3 parts air to 1 part fuel, and in severe cases, equal parts of fuel and air (1 : 1) are needed. Much of this enriched fuel mixture is never burned; some goes out the exhaust and some finds its way into the oil, where it has a diluting effect and upsets the protective qualities of the lubricant. Much of it also ends up as engine deposits of one kind or another. If there was a way to avoid some of this fuel inefficiency during the cold start, we would be well on our way toward that long-lasting, fuel-saving engine. Limiting the use of the choke during warm-up is one way:

An example of the effect on fuel economy of the use of the choke during the warm-up is given in Figure 16. During the first cycle when the engine was cold, the choke had to be pulled out fully, giving a fuel consumption of about 11 mile/gal. As the engine gradually warmed up, the fuel evaporation gradually improved and the choke could be pushed home. Eventually, after 12 cycles or so, the fuel economy improved to about 20 mile/gal. This effect is almost entirely due to the poor quality of the mixture supplied to the engine. Had some form of quick-heating device been in use, then the number of cycles needed to achieve fully warmed-

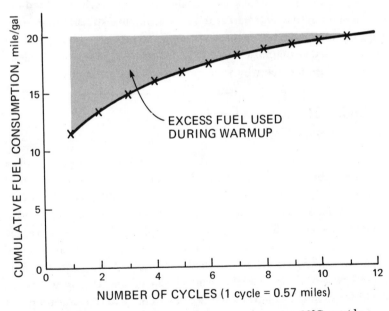

Figure 16. Fuel consumption during warm-up at $-10°C$ outside temperature.

up fuel economy would have been greatly reduced. Ideally and with a perfect mixture the fully warmed-up economy would have been reached after the first cycle.

Although most automobiles are equipped with devices that do assist in helping the engine heat faster and thus allow a more efficient, leaner mixture of fuel (thermostat, heat riser valve, thermostat-controlled fans, and so on), they fall far short of being capable of heating the engine to normal operating temperature within the above-stated ideal conditions of one cycle or .57 miles. Starting with a cold engine, some cars will still be spitting, stalling, hesitating, and in general having a tough go of it after being driven only .57 miles. There are, however, some devices that, even though they are not "quick-heating," can offer substantial help in our efforts to get the engine as warm as possible as fast as possible. Indeed they are probably the most overlooked products on the automotive aftermarket today and, in our estimation, are perhaps the most valuable engine-extending and economy-boosting items available for consumer use. Let's take a look at these inexpensive engine life extenders and see why your car shouldn't be without one.

Engine Heaters—They Can Turn Cold Starts Warm

As we have already seen, anything that shortens the time it takes for an engine to warm up will also lengthen the time the engine lives and will enhance its fuel economy potential. Cooling-system thermostats, manifold heat riser valves, thermostat-controlled fans, and even radiator covers all play a very important role in the engine warm-up cycle. But what if we never had to warm the car up? What if it was always warm? What if we never had to go through the cold-start routine? Think of all the gas that could be saved and engine wear that could be avoided. Unfortunately we can't eliminate the warm-up period, but we can cut down on the amount of time needed for the engine to warm. In fact we can cut that time dramatically with the aid of an item that will prove to be the most valuable add-on purchase you can make.

If you have ever been to Alaska or some of our colder areas stateside, you have probably noticed cars with an electric plug-in cord dangling from the front of their grills. These cords are for engine or oil heaters. In cold areas, many hotels, motels, apartments, and business or public parking areas have receptacles for these plugs at each parking place. The driver simply parks his car, plugs into the receptacle, and walks away, knowing his engine will be warm when he goes back to start it.

Engine coolant and engine oil heaters have been around for a long time, but except for motorists living in extremely cold portions of the country, they have been ignored by the majority of the driving public. This is unfortunate. They probably can do more to extend engine life, give better gas mileage, allow troublefree starts on the coldest of mornings, promote longer spark plug, oil, and filter life, reduce engine deposits and emissions—the list goes on—than any other single item available today. It is a crime of major proportions that they are not included as standard equipment on every new car, or at least offered as an option. Why have they been so ignored? Perhaps most drivers (yourself included?) are just not aware of them and the potential they have. Perhaps many car owners have heard of them but rationalize that they are meant only for cars located in cold climates. Nothing could be further from the truth. Engine or engine oil heaters can be used beneficially by the vast majority of the car-owning population, regardless of whether you live in Alaska or Arizona. The only difference between hot and cold climates will be in the amount of benefits received.

Whether you live in Minnesota or Miami, the car still gets cold overnight, although of course much more so in Minnesota. But in either locale the engine must still be warmed to normal operating temperature, the main difference being the amount of warming required. If the overnight low in Miami is 60°F while in Minnesota it is −10°F, the Minnesota car will have to warm itself 70° to be on a par with the Miami car. From that point both cars still must raise the coolant tem-

perature another 150 + ° to reach full warmth. This is why the engine
heater, regardless of climate, can be a valuable tool. It will keep the
engine coolant much warmer than the overnight low temperature and
in doing so will keep most of the engine warm also. It substantially
reduces the number of degrees of heat the engine itself must provide
to raise its temperature into the efficiency range.

Oil dipstick heaters or warmers do as their name implies: They keep
the oil warm. These simple heating elements replace your conventional
oil dipstick and by keeping the oil warm aid considerably in the cold
start. They are also useful in preventing the formation of condensation
in the oil and thus are a barrier against engine rust. Both engine oil
heaters and engine coolant heaters require conventional electrical outlets to function.

There are many types of engine heaters. Some plug into the engine
block itself, others use the lower radiator hose as the access point to
the engine coolant, while others hook into the car heater return line.
Most cause the coolant to circulate throughout the cooling system,
ensuring warmth for even the most remote engine parts. The nice
thing about most engine heaters is that they are not expensive and
require only moderate mechanical expertise to install. Once on the car
you just plug them in as required. Most coolant type warmers run in
the 12- to 25-dollar range; oil dipstick warmers can be purchased for
as little as five dollars. Cheap prices for the benefits derived.

Try to purchase a unit that has a thermostat control. This way it will
only heat up when the coolant temperature dictates, turning on and
off automatically as heat is needed, much like the heater blower on
your house furnace. If you purchase one without a thermostat—that
is, one that is on continually—plug it into a timer switch (available at
most hardware stores) and set the timer to come on at a preselected
time. As most engine coolant heaters take about three or four hours
to heat the coolant, setting the timer to come on three to four hours
before you plan to leave will save electricity while warming the engine
and the coolant to the heater's maximum ability.

In almost all water-cooled engines the coolant affects only the top part of the engine, and though much of this heat will seep into the lower part (bearings, crankshaft, and so on) and warm it, too. Cheap extra protection can be provided by a dipstick heating element. This ensures that the oil and lower engine parts will also be warm. An oil heating unit combined with an engine coolant heater ensures that you will be getting prompt and efficient oil circulation to pre-warmed engine parts. In short, you will be turning that cold start into a warm one.

Hastened warm-up period, particularly in sub-zero temperatures, and virtual elimination or reduced use of the choke means reduced wear rates when compared to a car in the same environment without the heaters. The heaters will pay for themselves in a short time in gas savings alone—the thousands of extra miles and years of engine use are your bonus.

Not necessary, but nice to have, especially when used with the above heaters, is a pre-moulded insulated blanket that will custom-fit over your engine. This seals engine heat in and prevents it from escaping to the atmosphere. Placed over the engine immediately after the car is retired for the night, the blanket will be very effective in trapping heat already present and will make the job of the engine heater that much easier. In an unheated garage, even on the coldest night, an insulated blanket will usually hold some of the engine's heat until the next morning. So even if you don't have an engine heater, a blanket can be of great help.

Anything you do that conserves the engine's heat will help in the next cool or cold start. Yes, even a 100-watt light bulb placed under the oil pan or next to the battery will help some.

By following the engine heater advice given here you will practically eliminate one of the most devastating periods of engine operation— the cold start and the miles that immediately follow. You really will have turned your cold starts warm. Close attention to this section and its recommendations should put you well on your way toward driving it forever.

This is all fine and good, you mutter, but what about the times when my car is in a parking lot or someplace where there are no plug-in facilities? There may be a way around this dilemma, but it involves adding another battery to your car. It can be carried in the trunk or, if you have room, in the engine compartment. The battery can provide the energy to run the engine heaters if it is adapted to some type of converter that will change its 12 volts into the 120 volts necessary to run the equipment. This way when you are out in the boondocks where no electrical facilities are available, you can just use your own. This means, of course, that the spare battery will have to be recharged occasionally after use.

A fifty-foot extension cord tucked away in the trunk is also a good idea. Many times electrical outlets are not placed where a car can go. The extra fifty feet of leeway provided by the extension cord can mean the difference between a cold and a warm start.

6

Gasolines—Can They
Affect Engine Wear?

They're All the Same, Aren't They?

We have seen that there are a number of things that can affect the warm-up cycle of a typical car. Some will prolong it; others, to the engine's benefit, will shorten it. Does the kind of gasoline you use have any effect on this warm-up cycle? You bet it does! Your gasoline has a direct bearing on the amount of time your car needs to reach normal operating temperature (NOT). The *more volatile* the gasoline, the *less time* required for warm-up. By volatility is meant how easily the gasoline will ignite.

But all gasolines are the same, aren't they, so what difference does it make what gas I use? No, all gasolines are *not* the same, and the brand of gasoline can make a startling difference in all aspects of engine performance. Gasoline volatility seems to be determined at the refinery and is directly related to the distilling process. The larger the percentage of gasoline that is distilled *below 100°C*, the more volatile the gasoline will be. Look at Figure 17 to see the difference gasoline volatility makes in the distance a car must travel to warm up. Remember, for our purposes the whole point here is to get the car warmed up as quickly as possible and thus minimize cold-engine wear. Using

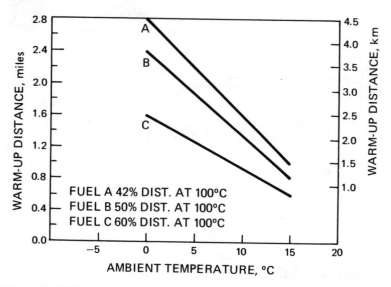

Figure 17. Effect of changes in the percentage of fuel distilled at 100°C (212°F) on the warm-up distance.

Fuel A, which has 42 percent distilled at 100°C (212°F), the car's warm-up distance is 4.3 km (2.7 miles), at 0°C (32°F) outside temperature. Using Fuel C, which has 60 percent distilled at 100°C (212°F), the warm-up distance is cut to 2.5 km (1.6 miles). This is very significant when we consider that most wear in an engine occurs when the engine is cold. So we see that the kind of gasoline we use can indeed play a vital role in determining how long it will take the car to warm up. This in turn has a direct effect on the entire engine wear process. It's too bad that volatility ratings of gasolines are not posted at the pump, but you *can* try different brands of gasoline to see how they affect your startability and warm-up cycle. Remember, there *is* a difference in gasolines, and only by experimentation can you find the really good ones.

◊　◊　◊

In your search for a good gasoline, it is a good idea to look for a brand that advertises custom blending by region or for various weather conditions. What may be an excellent gasoline under milder summer conditions may fail miserably in more demanding winter weather. Region- or climate-blended gasolines are fortified with additional additives to ensure proper engine operation under a variety of conditions.

A gasoline with a proven fuel-system cleaning additive (detergent) is a must. The detergent effectiveness can be seen and measured in fewer deposits in the carburetor and fuel system. The upper cylinder area of the engine also benefits. Eliminate deposits and you eliminate one source of wear. Your gasoline should have a fuel system cleaner in it. Of course, the custom-blended gasolines mentioned above may also have a detergent cleaner.

In their excellent book *Fuel Economy of the Gasoline Engine*, Blackmore and Thomas detail the effect fuel additives have on deposit formation. They mention that some of the more

> sensitive areas for deposit formation are carburetor throttle bodies, air bushes in carburetor idle and progression systems, positive crankcase ventilation (PCV) valves and exhaust gas recirculation (EGR) systems. Deposit build-up in any of these areas can have a substantial effect on air/fuel ratio and hence on fuel economy and emissions.

The upshot of this is that anything that can adversely affect the air/fuel ratio, fuel economy, and emissions will also have a deleterious effect on engine life. They go on to say that

> the adverse effects of carburetor deposits can readily be demonstrated in laboratory bench engine tests in which crankcase blowby

gases and exhaust gases are recirculated to the carburetor to accelerate deposit build-up. For example, in a standard carburetor cleanliness test procedure using a Ford Escort engine at TRC, increases in fuel consumption and exhaust emissions can readily be correlated with the build-up of throttle body deposits.

Look at Figure 18 for a graphic demonstration of how fuel consumption and emissions increase as carburetor deposits build up—and this is after only seven hours of test time.

It follows, therefore, that control of deposits by means of fuel additives offers benefits not only to the user but also to the community. This then is the background to the development of a new class of cleanliness additive which not only prevents deposit formation but also removes pre-formed deposits. In addition, a second-generation additive controls inlet valve deposit formation, an area in which the carburetor detergent is ineffective.

So we see then that gasoline is not just gasoline but includes a complex and precise blending of additives that have a positive effect on your car's engine. But you must remember that not all gasolines have all the additives, nor do they have them in the same amounts. In fact, some of the bargain basement brands may have no additives at all and should be assiduously avoided. For reducing engine wear and the wear of associated fuel system components, the additive content of the gasoline becomes just as important as, if not more than, the gasoline itself.

When we talk of trying different brands of gasoline we are not just "whistling Dixie." Regardless of what you have been told (all gasolines are the same, they all come out of the same storage tank, and so on), there are distinct differences among many brands. The differences come from the quality of the refining process. Perhaps you are now saying "Sure, I may change brands, but what difference will it make, because Brand A, which I am now using, is 90 octane and so is Brand

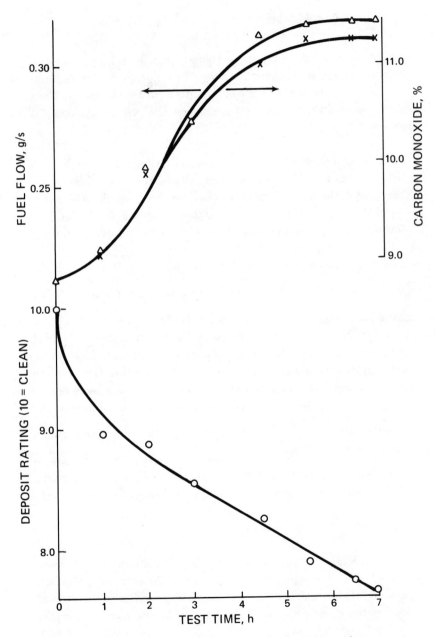

Figure 18. Fuel consumption, emissions, and carburetor deposits.

105

B, the one I am thinking about trying?" It will make a difference because no two gasolines are the same. Even though the octane numbers on the pump are the same, the performance each gasoline gives may be quite different, due to the manner in which the gasoline was refined,

and a discriminating motorist driving a critical car can, therefore, often detect the difference between two gasolines which have the same RON (Research Octane Number) number, i.e., the motorist is able to distinguish between gasolines which differ in MON (Motor Octane Number) or in RON of the more volatile portion.

What this means is that although the combined octane ratings of the gasolines—that is, the $\dfrac{R + M}{2}$ number we see posted at the pump—may both average out at 90 octane, *it is the amount or the octane rating of the more volatile portion of the gasoline that will affect performance the most.* So if you buy a gasoline that has a high octane rating for its most volatile portion (the portion that distills first in the refining process) and the one you have been using has a lower octane for that same volatile portion, then, even though the combined octane of both gasolines $\left(\dfrac{R + M}{2}\right)$ is 90, you can tell the difference between the two when using them in your car. Your engine is responsive to the octane of the most volatile portion of the gasoline removed in the refining process. Do experiment with different brands—no two are the same.

◇ ◇ ◇

What is octane? Octane is a measure of the gasoline's ability to resist engine knock. It is represented as a number; the higher the number, the better the fuel can resist knock. Thus a 95 octane gas would prevent knock better than an 89 octane gas. The number we see posted on the pump is commonly referred to as the pump octane or the $\dfrac{R + M}{2}$

octane. This is simply the Research Octane Number plus the Motor Octane Number divided by two. It is the number most motorists are familiar with.

Octane can be of vital importance in that it makes the gas capable of running an engine smoothly, without engine knock. This is important because engine knock, run-on, and upper cylinder noise due to using too low an octane fuel can cause eventual engine damage. Always make certain the gasoline you are using has sufficient octane to run your engine without knock.

Engine knock and run-on (the car continues to run after the engine is turned off) have been an all-too-common problem with many of the newer cars running on unleaded fuel. Almost all of the trouble could be traced to the low-octane unleaded fuels on the market. The smart motorist who used an octane booster didn't have this problem and his engine functioned smoothly. The recent advent of the super-premium unleaded fuels with a much higher octane rating has solved this problem for the most part. If you are still having a problem with engine knock and run-on and are still using a regular unleaded, switch to the new premium unleaded and your problems will probably disappear.

As an engine gets older and the wear process grinds out its eventual toll, it will require a higher-octane gasoline than when it was new. By forestalling the onset of engine senility you can continue to use, and get good performance from, the octane gasoline recommended for the car when it was new. An older engine usually requires a higher-octane gasoline than does its new counterpart if a comparable level of performance is desired.

Fuels that have a higher sulfur content will, upon burning, produce acids that eat at cylinder walls and pistons. They can also leave an abrasive residue that can cause wear in moving parts. This is important for diesel owners because low-grade diesel is sometimes heavy with sulfur. Purchase only the highest grade diesel fuel and you protect your car against sulfur damage. (This can also be true of gasoline, but to a much lesser degree.)

One of the main complaints newer-car owners have concerns the unpleasant rotten-egg odor that is sometimes prevalent inside and outside the car. This odor has become even more noticeable with the introduction of 3-way catalytic converters that treat hydrocarbon, carbon-monoxide, and nitrous-oxide emissions. The smell can be traced to the third, or nitrous-oxide, stage of emissions treatment.

Where does the smell come from? From sulfur in the gasoline—and all gasolines have some sulfur. After gasoline is burned in the engine, the exhaust finds its way to the catalytic converter where it undergoes a chemical reaction. The converted sulfur is released to the atmosphere in the form of hydrogen sulfide (H_2S), a gas to which the human nose is very sensitive. The more oxygen present in the converter, the stronger the smell. If you are plagued by the rotten-egg syndrome, take solace in the fact that the sulfur isn't harmful to the car or the emissions system, even though that won't help your suffering nose. Here are some things you can do to make breathing a little more pleasant:

- Experiment with different brands of gasoline. One may contain less sulfur than another.
- Try an emissions-control-system cleaner, available at most auto parts stores and service stations.
- Go easy on the full-throttle accelerations. Much of a full charge of gasoline suddenly dumped into the engine remains unburned. Raw gasoline that comes into direct contact with the catalytic converter intensifies the odor.
- Be certain ignition timing is set correctly.
- Ask a technician whether recalibrating the engine computer or altering the air/fuel mixture might help.

When testing different brands or octanes of gasoline, be sure to give the gasoline a fair test. The tank should be relatively empty when you fill up with the new brand so that what little is left of the old gas won't affect your judgment of the qualities of the new.

Okay, so you live in the far north and don't have facilities for a car engine heater hookup and there's no garage or shelter to protect your car—can you still be assured of good startability in cold weather? Other than moving to a warmer climate, there are a number of things you can do to help. A fully charged battery is something no Northerner would be caught without, so we won't mention that. It will pay to check the various brands of gasoline in your area for their BTU (heat) content and volatility—the higher the BTU's, the better the volatility and the easier the cold weather starts. Although most major brands are similar in their BTU ratings, some *are* a bit higher than others. Buy the gas with the highest rating, for in sub-zero temperatures this "little bit" can make a big difference. You'll have to call the suppliers or write the company to get the BTU content but it's worth it. (Another very important cold weather starting factor, choice of oil, is discussed on pp. 60–61.)

Chances are you've heard someone complain at one time or another about filling up with a "bad batch" of gasoline. Perhaps it has happened to you. You fill the tank and the car doesn't seem to perform as well; you attribute it to a bad batch of gasoline. Chances are you were right, it *was* a bad batch of gasoline; and chances are you bought some offbeat brand. Many offbeat cheap brands are literally the bottom of the barrel and contain the sediments and water that settle on the bottom. Are all brands of gasoline the same and do all receive the same storage care? Bet you didn't go back and buy that brand again!

Don't buy gas while a tanker truck is filling up the station's tanks. The gas going into the underground tanks could stir up any sediment present, which could end up in your tank.

Except when experimenting with different brands, try not to run your tank down too close to empty. The gasoline is more likely to pick up sediment, rust, or water that may be there and carry them into the engine. This is doubly important if the tank is near empty and the car has been sitting a long time.

Keeping the gas tank on the full side during winter months will help eliminate condensation buildup inside the tank. This water in the gas doesn't make it any easier to start the car on cold mornings and encourages fuel-tank rusting and ice buildup in the gasoline itself.

◊ ◊ ◊

Gasohol, or fuels with up to 10 percent alcohol content, will burn somewhat cleaner than straight gasoline. If these are available, experiment with them. If you can get equivalent performance from these alcohol-enhanced fuels, they may be worth using because of the slightly reduced engine deposits of the cleaner-burning alcohol. One major drawback to alcohol fuels—they are usually quite a bit more expensive than straight gasoline.

Use of the ethanol- and methanol-blended gasolines is becoming more common each year, and some states and cities even require their use during anticipated high-smog periods. Denver, for instance, has mandated the use of alcohol fuels during winter months to help cut down on air pollution, and some cities in Arizona have recently followed Denver's cue. Where law demands, you must use these fuels in your car regardless of the type of vehicle you drive.

But many people are concerned about the effects of these alcohol-blended fuels on their cars' engines. Can these fuels, which help clean up our air, do damage to the engines of cars that use them?

In the past, methanol- or ethanol-enhanced gasolines were viewed suspiciously because their use was synonymous with accelerated wear of certain fuel-system parts. But most newer cars have fuel systems built with special materials resistant to alcohol degradation, and many can safely use these fuels providing the alcohol content doesn't exceed 10 percent.

However, manufacturers that permit the use of alcohol-blended fuels caution that if the fuel makes the car hard to start or if performance is noticeably affected, you should go back to using straight gasoline.

The best answer to whether or not you can use alcohol-blended fuels in your car remains the same as it has been in the past: Refer to your owner's manual. That is the only way to know which fuels can safely be fed to the car. For example, a Thunderbird owner's manual says that you can use these blends, but then attaches a number of provisos. Each car manufacturer has different feelings about using alcohol blends, and some, such as Subaru, still prohibit their use entirely.

◊ ◊ ◊

As we have seen, gasoline octane is very important to your car's health, mileage, and overall engine life. Inadequate octane over extended periods can only do harm. But even though the figures posted at the pump indicate that the gasoline is of sufficient octane for your car, you still may not be getting the octane you need. How is this possible? Because what you see listed on the pump $\left(\text{the } \dfrac{R\ +\ M}{2} \text{ octane number} \right)$ *may not* be what you get in your tank.

I participated in a week-long TV series on gasoline octane in the Tucson area. Samples of gasoline were taken from various gasoline stations around town and their octane (as posted on the pump) was recorded. The octanes of the samples were then tested at the University of Arizona testing lab. (This is the same lab, incidentally, that tests gasolines for the state and gives the rating to each gasoline dispensed.) Almost every one of these samples proved to be lower in actual octane than the figures posted at the pump. In one case, the octane of a sample turned out to be almost four points lower than the station had posted! The unwary motorist, expecting the full octane (the *price* was for the full octane) was, in reality, getting substantially lower, and the car's performance undoubtedly suffered as a consequence. Thinking that "it couldn't be the gas," many of these unsuspecting souls may have looked for the cause of erratic engine performance elsewhere, costing them time, money, and engine wear.

Can this happen in your town? Probably, and chances are it *is* happening right now. In lieu of a full-scale investigation and monthly checks of station octane, what is the motorist to do to guard against this kind of ripoff? Buy at a reputable station. Keep your senses tuned for any change in the automobile's performance. If the gasoline gives poor service, don't go back to that station. Ask the state to run a check on the octane at that particular station. Nothing will make an errant station toe the line as quickly as a stiff fine. In the final analysis it is you the motorist who has to make the ultimate choice. Be critical. Listen to your car—it will talk back to you and let you know if what is posted on the pump is actually what is going into your tank.

Leaded Gasoline—Essential Succor for Older Cars?

In a January 1988 syndicated column, I answered my readers' most asked questions:

How will the Environmental Protection Agency's (EPA) order requiring refiners to reduce the amount of lead in gasoline affect the millions of cars and engines that were designed to run on leaded gas and what, if any, precautions should be taken?

Since the EPA ordered a gradual phaseout of lead in gasoline for environmental and health reasons, the lead content has dropped from a high of about 2.5 grams per gallon (gpg) to the current maximum allowable 0.1 gpg. Leaded gasoline itself has become more difficult— if not impossible in some areas—to find. For years tetraethyl lead (TEL) has been used by refiners as an economical way to boost octane. It has also lubricated the upper cylinder area of the car's engine. It is the lack of lubrication that worries car owners.

During the combustion process TEL in the form of lead salts is deposited on or around the valves, valve guides and, most important, the valve seats. It acts as a buffer against metal-to-metal contact as the valves close against their seats. Gasoline exploding in the cylinders constantly replenishes the lead coating. Without lead, valve seats can wear rapidly and recede into the cylinder head. If this happens, engine compression and performance suffer and can only be restored with a costly engine rebuild.

Is the current—January 1989—0.1 gpg enough to protect valve parts against premature wear? That depends on the vehicle and how it is driven. If used moderately in urban areas, a vehicle can do quite well with low-lead gasoline. But if the car is driven at higher speeds or pulls trailers or climbs hills regularly or is operated at high engine rpm or in high heat conditions, then 0.1 gpg is not adequate. Most farm vehicles, construction equipment, large trucks, buses, mobile travel homes and even some pickup trucks, along with passenger cars that are driven "hard," fall into this category.

But there is a catch: 0.1 gpg is the maximum lead content allowed by law. Many refiners actually add less, as there is no minimum standard for what constitutes leaded gasoline. Indeed, the gas you are using now, although technically called leaded, may just barely be so. There is no way to tell at the pump. But will even that small amount eventually be phased out?

James Caldwell, chief of the fuels section of the Office of Mobile Resources at the EPA, says that although the proposal for a total ban on leaded gasoline is still on the shelf, the EPA at this time has "no final plans to proceed with a ban on leaded gasoline."

If your car was made prior to 1975, it does not have hardened valve parts and should use leaded gasoline. (Hardened valve parts are used in newer cars that burn unleaded gasoline and don't need valve lubrication.) Ford Motor Co. recommends leaded gasoline for all its cars with soft metal valve parts built before 1975. General Motors says all its cars built before 1971 should use leaded gasoline. (Owners of pickup trucks and other vehicles should consult their owner's manuals for fuel type.)

If your car does not have hardened valve parts:

- Continue to use leaded gasoline as long as possible.
- Monitor driving habits closely. Keep speeds under 55 mph. Avoid

driving in high heat for prolonged periods or overheating the engine. Don't pull trailers or carry heavy loads. Keep engine rpm to a maximum of 2,500. Don't gun the motor at idle or use full-throttle accelerations.

• Consider the use of a lead-substitute additive available at many service stations and auto-parts stores. They offer some protection against valve-seat wear.

Testing by the EPA and Department of Agriculture showed that lead-substitute additives decreased valve wear when used according to manufacturer's directions. However, they didn't halt wear completely. When another test was done using four times the recommended amount, valve wear was stopped completely.

• If your engine must be rebuilt, hardened valve parts should be used in the rebuilding. The parts may cost a bit more, but they will enable your car to run safely on *unleaded* gas.

Much of what I wrote in that column was echoed eight months later in an EPA notice published in the October 7, 1988, *Federal Register*, which also contained additional pertinent information for owners of vehicles using leaded gasoline:

• Leaded gasoline at the 0.10 gplg (grams per liquid gallon) level is adequate to avoid valve recession in most . . . engines.

• Exclusive use of unleaded gasoline can lead to valve recession in many engines designed for leaded gasoline when operated at medium to high engine speeds.

• Some leaded gasoline could have significantly less lead than 0.10 gplg.

• Leaded gasoline demand continues to drop. Many refiners are planning to drop leaded gasoline in selected regions of the country . . . Leaded gasoline is expected to be only about 10 percent of total gasoline usage in the 1990s.

• Non-lead additives have significant potential as substitutes for lead. . . .

• Unleaded gasoline of sufficient octane may be used if an engine has the following:

- Hard steel valve seats; or
- Soft valve seats, but is used exclusively for light-duty, low-speed operations; or
- Soft valve seats, but is a low-RPM engine (less than 1,700 revolutions per minute).

The notice continues with this advice for areas where no leaded gasoline is available:

In situations where only unleaded gasoline is available, and for engines that will be vulnerable to valve-seat recessions, take the following steps:
- Reduce heavy loads on the engine by shifting down and reducing engine speed (i.e., take longer to do tasks that put a heavy strain on the engine);
- Enrich the carburetor air-to-fuel mixture;
- Keep engines in good repair and follow proper maintenance requirements, particularly with respect to the cooling system, and keep engines free from attachments that can restrict air flow and trap heat;
- Use an alternative valve lubricating additive, where available, during periods of heavy use to reduce the risk or extent of damage;
- Do a valve job sooner than planned. Install hard steel valve sets at the next engine overhaul. If the engine has valve rotators, have them removed or disabled.

And finally, "At this time, the EPA does not have any final plans to ban leaded gasoline, but will continue to aggressively evaluate both the health effects of lead and the potential for engine damage. . . ."

Here are some additional suggestions.

- It's not news that older cars that were meant to use leaded premium gasoline are having a tough time of it. Ethyl, premium, or super leaded gasolines are, for the most part, non-existent. In fact, it's getting hard to find plain old leaded regular.

• Any older car that was made to run on *leaded premium* should use one of the following combinations of gasoline and/or additives: leaded regular with unleaded premium plus an octane booster; leaded regular with an octane booster; leaded regular plus an octane booster and a lead-substitute additive; and, finally, the one to use if you have doubts: leaded regular with unleaded premium plus a lead-substitute additive and an octane booster if needed. If leaded regular isn't available, then use unleaded premium with a lead-substitute additive.

• Keep one thing in mind when trying these various combinations: The way your car reacts to any particular mix is the key. If it pings, it needs more octane, so you should add an octane booster or more premium unleaded to the mix. But always try to keep the leaded-regular content at least 50 percent of the total, because the engine needs lead protection.

Fuel Injection

One of the automotive buzzwords of the '80s, and one that will be a household word as the '90s roll around, is fuel injection. To be more specific, let's make that electronic fuel injection. We hear or read about it almost every day in new-car ads extolling the virtues of their electronic fuel-injected engines. What is fuel injection and what should be done to keep it operating at peak efficiency?

Just ten years ago fuel injection was found exclusively in slick, imported sports sedans; today the majority of all new vehicles are fuel-injected. Fuel injection is simply a method of supplying fuel to an engine so it will run. It is rapidly replacing the faithful old carburetor as the main fuel-supply system because it is more efficient and economical and allows the engine to perform closer to its designed potential.

Typically, an electronic fuel-injection system must have an electric fuel pump near or in the gas tank. It delivers pressurized fuel to the engine. This fuel must pass through a filter, just as in a carbureted car. It is critical that the filter be clean and changed according to the manufacturer's instructions. Dirty fuel can immobilize an injection system—and the car—very quickly. Fuel injection is much more sensitive to fuel quality and cleanliness than a carburetor is.

Once the pressurized fuel passes through the filter it goes into a long tubular affair called the distributor pipe. This pipe's job is to distribute the fuel through smaller connecting tubes to each engine cylinder. As the fuel is fed through these tubes, it comes in touch with the fuel injector. In other systems the fuel passes directly from the fuel filter into a throttle-body arrangement where it is mixed with air and passed into the intake manifold.

The fuel injector, a miniature hose nozzle-like device, electronically injects fuel into the engine. This can be done in a variety of ways depending on the system installed in the car. The current systems are single point, throttle body and multiport or multipoint injection.

Single point means there is just one point where the fuel is injected. Throttle body means that the point of injection is on the throttle body, a unit that sits on top of the intake manifold. In both systems fuel is injected either through one or two injectors into the throttle body where it is mixed with air, passed into the intake manifold and on to the engine's cylinders.

Multipoint means there is more than one point where fuel is injected. Typically, an injector is located directly above each engine-intake valve where it feeds fuel to each cylinder. Multiport means the same thing as multipoint, that is, there are individual ports (or points), usually above the intake valves, where fuel is injected.

A variation of the multiport and multipoint systems is the sequential-port fuel-injection system. Instead of giving all cylinders a shot of fuel at the same time, this system synchronizes the delivery with each intake stroke. It is usually considered the best and most precise fuel-injection system.

Fuel-injection systems are quite dependable but must be kept sparkling clean to perform properly. If you live in a dusty area, change fuel filters more often. And no matter where you live, use nothing but high-quality, high-detergent gasoline which will keep the injectors clean. As an extra safeguard, occasional use of a fuel-injector cleaner is O.K.

Poor-quality gasoline in a fuel-injection system acts like an overload of cholesterol in the blood stream. Excessive cholesterol will eventually clog the arteries and restrict the flow of blood to the heart. Low-detergent, cheap or dirty fuel in a fuel-injected car, when ingested by the engine over a long period, leaves deposits on the fuel injectors. This buildup retards and changes the spray pattern of gasoline injected into the cylinders. Restricted injectors can cause poor starts, stumbling, rough running, and loss of power.

At one time the problem of poor quality, low-detergent gasolines became so serious that General Motors asked the major oil companies to make higher quality, injector-compatible, high-detergent gasolines. Most major oil companies responded with a high-detergent gasoline that keeps injectors from fouling and, in many cases, actually cleans up established injector deposits.

If you have a fuel-injected car, don't use cheap, offbeat brands of gasoline. You will pay the price in poor engine performance, reduced fuel economy, and heightened engine deterioration. Look for major brands that advertise the high-detergent qualities of their fuels. Union 76, Chevron, Exxon, Shell, Mobil, Arco, Amoco, Sunoco, and Texaco are but a few that do.

Gasoline Additives—Liquid Dope or Liquid for Dopes?

Everyone loves to get in on the act—purchasing gasoline additives in one form or another, dumping them in the gas tank, and hoping they will be the magic elixir they have been searching for. By purchasing a good-quality gasoline in the first place you will save money because that quality gasoline will contain everything the additive has and more. Anti-icing compounds in cold weather, rust and corrosion preventives, anti-wear (engine) and carburetor compounds, and detergents that keep the carburetor, intake valves, and emissions and ventilation systems clean are all part of a good gasoline. Will the additive you buy do any good? Except in isolated instances, probably not—you're just throwing money away.

How about fuel system cleaners? You've seen many of them advertised on TV, radio, and in print. Are they any good? Can they do any harm? Consider the advice Chrysler Corporation gives in one of its new-car owner's manuals: "Indiscriminate use of fuel system cleaning agents should be avoided. Many of these materials intended for gum and varnish removal may contain active solvents or similar ingredients that can be harmful to gasket and diaphragm materials used in fuel system component parts." The key words, of course, are "indiscriminate use." You should totally avoid using such cleaners; if you insist, use them only occasionally.

One type of gasoline additive that can be beneficial is fuel-injector cleaners. Of course, they should be used on cars equipped with fuel injection, but they won't hurt carbureted cars, either. These injector cleaners came on the market a few years ago, when car makers were being plagued by problems with fuel-injector clogging. And although the advent of high-detergent, clean gasolines has curtailed their use, an occasional can of fuel-injector cleaner won't do any harm.

Another gasoline additive that wasn't around when this book originally was written is a lead substitute gasoline additive. These came on the market soon after the EPA's decision to reduce the content of lead in leaded gasoline to its present maximum of 0.1 grams per gallon. They were formulated to take the place of the missing lead. Lead is needed in older engines to lubricate various valve parts especially the valve seats. Without proper lead protection, valve seats in older cars can recess and eventually cost the owner the price of a rebuilt engine.

◊ ◊ ◊

One occasion when you may want to (and should) use some type of gasoline additive (preferably an octane booster) is when traveling in Mexico. Low-octane Pemex gas can play havoc with even the best-tuned engine. An octane booster will ensure better engine performance and protection. A top cylinder lubricant (top oil) added to the gas or oil is also another reasonable precaution under these circumstances.

◊ ◊ ◊

For winter driving it may be a good practice to add a gasoline volatility improver or an octane booster to your gas tank—*if you need it*. The more volatile a gasoline is, the more easily it will burn. If you have trouble getting your car to fire up on cold days and all mechanical details are okay, then the problem may lie with the gasoline itself. If changing brands has proved ineffective, then some type of improver may do the trick. If it works it will be well worth the dollar or two because of less aggravation and reduced wear on the engine.

◊ ◊ ◊

The final test of any gasoline will be how it performs in your car. A discerning driver will be able to tell the difference between brands, particularly between quality brands and low-priced freeway specials. This is the ultimate criterion. Good performance, engine feel and idle, fast starts in all conditions, smooth acceleration—all are desirable attributes of any gasoline. Find that perfect blend for your car and stick with it.

◊ ◊ ◊

Some car owners like to put a gallon or so of diesel fuel in their tanks at each fillup; in fact, some gas stations sell motor fuel that already contains 4 to 5 percent diesel. Claims for using diesel as a gasoline additive run anywhere from better mileage to smoother performance to longer engine life. Advice here: Put diesel in diesels; put gasoline in gasoline engines; and don't mix the two. Regardless of claims, not enough is known about the long-term effects of using a diesel mix in a gasoline engine. Stay with what the manufacturer meant for your engine and be on the safe, not the sorry, side.

Your car is a lot like your body. Genetic factors play a large part in determining how long you will live. If longevity runs in your family, then chances are good that you will enjoy a long life. Your body's longevity factors are determined by your mother and father, who are, essentially, the factory that built you. Many of your car's longevity factors are also built in at the factory; just as some people are built better, so are some cars. Given equal treatment, these cars will last longer than others. Over and above genetic factors, how you live, what you eat, the care you give yourself, the exercise you get, your job, and the like all play parts in determining your life expectancy. Your car again is no different. The treatment it receives, the way it is driven, the jobs it performs, and the quality of food (gasoline, oil, lubricants, and additives) it receives are all very important in determining just how long it will last. Following the advice in this book will guarantee the best overall program of automotive longevity practices for your car.

7

Engine- and Car-Saving Options and Add-Ons

The Fuel System

Two excellent items that are highly recommended for any car equipped with an automatic choke are a hand choke conversion kit and a hand throttle. These units are inexpensive and easy to install, and can be purchased at any auto supply store. A hand choke allows fingertip dash-mounted control of the carburetor butterfly or choke valve. During a cold start the driver need only apply as much choke as is needed to keep the engine running smoothly. Prudent hand choke use will ensure proper mixture at all stages of the warm-up and will virtually do away with the over-rich mixtures commonly associated with the automatic choke. Any possibility of the choke's sticking is also eliminated, along with a host of other bothersome and harmful automatic choke problems. By ensuring the engine a proper mixture during warm-up, oil dilution and deposit formation from unburned fuel are minimized. A hand choke, if used properly, will reduce engine wear and improve gas mileage when compared to the automatic choke. Another outstanding benefit of the hand choke is that as the car works through its warm-up cycle, the driver can constantly lessen the amount of choke needed, the main criterion being how the engine is running under each setting. This allows the driver to complete his choke cycle much sooner than with an automatic choke. If you would like to take a major step toward reducing engine wear, by all means equip your car with a hand choke.

If you are the forgetful type, it might pay to have a warning light installed along with the hand choke. The light will come on when the choke is engaged. This way you'll be less liable to forget that the choke is on. However, with a little practice, driving with a hand choke becomes second nature and you learn to push it in as engine performance dictates.

In combination with a hand choke, a hand throttle is also a good investment. This is simply a hand-adjustable dash-mounted control of the accelerator pedal. It comes in handy during the cold-start and warm-up cycle when slightly higher engine speeds may be desired. With the hand throttle the exact engine idle speed can be set and will hold there until released by the driver. Once the engine is sufficiently warmed, the throttle can be pushed back in to obtain normal idling speed.

If your car does not have an "in-line" fuel filter, by all means have one installed. The porous metal-type filters commonly built into the carburetor don't do a good enough job of keeping dirt from entering the carburetor and engine. An in-line paper filter element will do a much better job. Always change fuel filters using the manufacturer's recommendations as a *minimum guide*—change much sooner if dusty conditions are encountered or if the gasoline you have been using is suspect.

If you are ever faced with the choice of fuel injection versus carburetion, it would be well to remember that, all other conditions being equal, fuel injection will serve the car owner better. The engine benefits from the accuracy with which fuel injection delivers the air/fuel charge to each cylinder. One of the main problems with carbureted engines is that some cylinders receive more fuel than the others; in a poorly designed intake manifold, this means some cylinder areas will be more deposit prone while others are fuel starved, which could cause valve burning. Fuel injection, although not perfect, allows a better and more equitable fuel mixture distribution, which results in a better-running, longer-lasting engine.

The Electrical System

The battery is the heart of your ignition and electrical system. The next time you need a battery, buy the highest ampere rated battery you can find. A fully charged, high-rated battery is possibly the most important part of the cold-start cranking cycle. The more power available, the faster the car will start under adverse conditions, and this means less wear on all components involved. As Eric Braithwaite noted, "When available battery energy was increased substantially, the engine startability was significantly improved." A "super" battery also ensures maximum ignition and spark voltages at all times; this translates to more complete combustion and less deposits. Although initial cash outlay is a bit more, you might consider one of the lifetime-guarantee batteries. They are about the highest-rated battery made and since you plan to keep the car for a long time, why worry about ever paying for a battery again?

The ignition coil seldom if ever needs replacement. In the event yours does, replace it with a high-voltage, high-capacity coil. This, in combination with a high-rated battery, will permit the hottest spark possible in the combustion chamber and allow fast, easy starts.

One good way to help beat the problem of engine deposit buildup is by getting more complete combustion of the fuel. This is especially important if you do a lot of stop-and-go or short-trip driving. How do you get better combustion? We have seen that the type of gasoline you use makes a difference; another way is to install the next *hottest* range spark plug in your engine the next time plugs have to be replaced. Go up only one heat range at a time. The manufacturer of your car had to choose a plug that was a compromise between city and highway driving and hot and cold weather. If cold weather or stop-and-go driving is heavy on your agenda, then the next hottest range plug may be just what the doctor ordered. Conversely, if you are on the road for 80 percent of your car's miles, or if you live in a hot climate, then one heat range *cooler* may be just what you are looking for.

Adding a capacitive discharge or electronic ignition can be very helpful if your car is not already so equipped. These units have proved they can extend spark plug, distributor, and valve life by ensuring a better quality spark at the cylinders. Combined with the products just discussed, this is the Cadillac of engine accessories. Although the claims for more miles per gallon attributed to these units are sometimes exaggerated, they are nevertheless a very valuable tool in the quest for more miles per car. A good investment, capacitive discharge or electronic ignition can easily be removed from the car in the event you should decide to sell it.

The Cooling System

Car cooling systems (should they be called heating systems?) are practically trouble- and service-free. Changing coolant and flushing the system occasionally are the only requirements, but because of its troublefree nature, it is an all-too-easy area to ignore.

The cooling system contains one of the most important wear-fighting items on the car—the thermostat. A properly functioning thermostat of the correct heat range is absolutely essential. The function of the thermostat is to force your engine to heat up faster, and the faster it heats up the less it will wear. When the engine is cold the thermostat remains closed, blocking the flow of coolant from the radiator to the engine and allowing the engine to heat up more rapidly. Once the desired temperature is reached (as pre-determined by the temperature rating of the thermostat), the thermostat opens and coolant is allowed to circulate throughout the engine. This opening and closing keeps the coolant at the desired temperature from that point on. Most thermostat temperature recommendations today call for a hot 212°F+ coolant temperature. This advice should be followed for older cars also, and the hottest thermostat recommended by the manufacturer should always be used.

You should be absolutely certain that: (1) Your car has a thermostat—no car should be without one. (2) It is the hottest one that can safely be used. (3) It is functioning properly. (Lukewarm heater air probably means the thermostat is stuck open; an engine that is constantly overheating may indicate the thermostat is stuck closed. If you have any doubt about its operation, replace it.)

It is a good idea to use some kind of radiator cover or blind in extremely cold weather (0°F and below) to assist the engine in warming up and keeping warm. On a very cold day, the thermostat—even though it is working properly—may not keep the engine warm enough because the cold outside air and the radiator fan are cooling the coolant faster than the engine can heat it. A piece of vinyl or even a chunk of cardboard placed in front of the radiator will hasten warm-up and help keep the engine temperature up. Under extremely cold conditions it may not even be necessary to remove it once the engine has warmed; merely slide it a bit to the side to permit some of the outside air to pass through. This is a judgment call, however, and the motorist must decide how much of the radiator should be covered. If you have an engine temperature gauge then you can adjust the cover to get the exact coolant temperature desired.

◇ ◇ ◇

While we're on the subject of radiators, it doesn't make very good sense that at the very time you are trying to warm your engine as fast as possible, the radiator fan is working equally hard to cool it. The last thing we need with a cold engine is the fan. Many new car manufacturers have recognized this dilemma, and thermostatically controlled fans are now appearing on new cars. These fans sense the temperature of the engine and only come on when a pre-designated temperature is reached. They are a valuable aid to engine life. If you don't have this type of fan—and unless you own a newer car, chances are you don't—an investment in one may be a good idea. Also available commercially are clutch drive and electric fans that the owner can control from inside the driver's compartment. These will do much the same job as the thermostat-controlled types.

Any addition to the engine, whether it is a mechanical device or a fluid additive, will affect the original intention of the engine. The point is to make sure the effect is a positive one. Each addition mentioned here will have a positive effect. For instance, a different fan will alter the heat balance of the engine but will do so in a positive manner (i.e., the fan won't run when the engine is cold, thus allowing for a reduced warm-up period). A number of so-called gas- and engine-saving devices claim positive benefits all around, but upon closer investigation extended use of these devices proves harmful. That's why they won't even be mentioned here.

The Intake and Exhaust Systems

It doesn't take a mechanic to know that the faster and more efficiently an engine rids itself of exhaust fumes, the better off it is. For this reason it's good economy to consider a dual exhaust system. The faster these contaminants are drawn from the engine, the less likely they are to hang around and form deposits. A dual exhaust system will get rid of spent gases more completely and will help the engine breathe easier.

Increased economy and prolonged engine life, along with a smoother-performing engine, are related benefits.

On newer cars with emissions control equipment, however, don't alter any portion of the exhaust system, since it is actually part of the emissions control system. Tampering with the exhaust configuration is illegal and can upset the delicate balance needed for the most efficient emissions control. Only attempt these modifications on pre-1975 cars.

A muffler should muffle engine noise and should also allow free and unimpeded exit of exhaust gases. The next time you need a muffler, investigate some of the low back pressure or performance types. Many of these have reached a nice compromise between noise level (about as quiet as the original) and back pressure (less than the original). Anything that eases engine back pressure will help the engine run easier, with the end result being that it also wears easier.

There is no doubt that some cars are just built better and last longer than other cars. These cars usually cost more at the time of initial purchase, but this extra value usually shows as time passes. Quality will stand the test of time. How many Mercedes will you find in the local junkyard?

Some engines, too, are better than others. The original factory design variations can make a big difference in total engine life, one of the most important designs being that of the intake manifold. Some intake manifolds are so poorly designed that the car has a hard time just idling; others permit the engine to purr like a kitten.

A high-performance intake manifold is an aftermarket item that may well be worth its weight in oil. One of the areas where many stock manifolds fall short is in the compromise design built in at the factory. Many engine problems, including rusting and accelerated wear, can be traced to a poorly designed intake manifold. Many designs do not allow the proper mixing and distribution of the fuel mixture to the cylinders. This causes rough idling and poor cold engine performance, all-too-common ailments for many cars. A custom, high-performance intake manifold can cure these problems and their offshoot ills of rapid deposit buildup, oil contamination, and accelerated wear. Although expensive, this engine-altering addition may be well worth it if your car exhibits some of the above tendencies, and you plan to keep the car for a while.

Headers are a hot-rod or racing innovation that has been around a long time. Essentially they are individual exhaust pipes for each cylinder. If you are into engine modifications, this should be high on your list. They will—besides giving the car a racy appearance—give exhaust gases the shortest path to the outside air, help engine economy and cleanliness, and add to engine life.

You can dress up your car a bit and add ever so slightly to engine efficiency by installing a scavenger tip on your tailpipe. This is nothing but a chrome-plated exhaust pipe extension with the opening pointing down. At higher speeds the down-fluted opening allows air passing under it to help draw fumes from the engine, relieving engine back pressure just a fraction.

The Engine and Transmission Lube Cases

Engine oil and transmission fluid coolers are, as their names suggest, add-on units that help keep the engine oil and transmission fluid cool. They can be very valuable if you do much high-speed, hot-weather driving or if you do a lot of towing. These severe service conditions will rapidly overheat an engine or transmission and cause increased oxidation of their lubricating fluids. The lower part of an engine depends entirely on the oil to cool it. Under severe service conditions, the oil can overheat, causing the lower engine to overheat. Transmission and oil coolers guard against this problem by keeping the fluids at a more acceptable temperature. Cooler fluids mean better heat removal from critical areas and more efficient engine and transmission working parts.

As we saw in Chapter 2, heat is the number-one enemy of transmission life. Operating an excessively hot transmission can destroy it in as little as half an hour. Anything you can do to keep it cool will pay dividends in longer life.

Abrasive wear due to extraneous grit is very common and considerable savings can sometimes be obtained by improving filtration of air and of lubricants. It is also important to ensure where possible that the wear debris itself is not abrasive. This cannot always be done, since most wear debris consists of oxide particles and most oxides are hard and abrasive. It is then necessary to remove the debris efficiently from the working area.

Besides providing the engine with an efficient oil filtration system, another excellent way to remove wear debris is by using magnetic drain plugs instead of the conventional ones. Magnetic drain plugs are simply replacement plugs for your oil pan, transmission, and rear axle lube cases that have a magnet in their center. As these plugs are in the mainstream of the lubricant movement or flow, they can easily pick up metallic wear debris and hold it there until the lubricants are either checked or changed. As we have seen, some of this wear debris may be particles of oxides, which are hard and abrasive. The magnetic plugs remove this debris, which, if left circulating, could do damage before being removed at the next lubricant change. Magnetic plugs are highly recommended not only for the oil drain pan but also for the transmission and differential.

◊ ◊ ◊

A number of years ago some auto supply houses carried magnesium element magnetic oil drain plugs. These were regular magnetized drain plugs with a stick of magnesium placed in the center. The function of the magnesium was to help neutralize any acid buildup in the oil. They may or may not be available anymore; if you can find this product, it is well worth the looking. We have seen how acid in the oil can damage an engine. Look at Figure 19 to see the effect that increasing the alkalinity (reducing the acidity) of the oil has on wear. The more alkaline the oil (within certain limits), the better it fights engine wear. From Figure 19 we see that as the alkalinity is increased, the relative wear rate is decreased. This speaks highly of using any product, such as magnesium element drain plugs or magnesium strips, that can offset acid contamination.

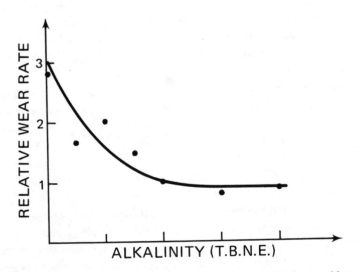

Figure 19. Total wear vs. alkalinity content using a highly basic additive treatment.

◊   ◊   ◊

A large-capacity oil filter is an excellent aftermarket investment. Current factory-installed filters are not really large enough to get the job done properly. This is especially true at the manufacturer's recommended extended (7,500 to 12,000 miles) oil-change intervals. The small filters are not adequate to handle the tremendous volume of oil that must pass through them. Many of these filters are probably operating in the bypass stage for much of the time, allowing oil to bypass the filter element because it has become clogged. A booster or large-capacity oil filter ensures adequate and complete filtering of the moving oil at all times; this is extremely important when there is a chance of abrasives being present.

Gauges

An add-on that no car should be without is the vacuum gauge. It is one of the most valuable pieces of equipment an owner can have on his car. A good-quality vacuum gauge can be purchased in the 20- to 30-dollar range; cheaper but still functional ones are available. (See Figure 20.)

If you are *really* interested in improving performance, fuel economy, driving habits, and engine life, then by all means purchase one of these valuable aids. A vacuum gauge does what you would think it would do: It measures engine vacuum. The higher the vacuum, the more efficiently the engine is operating. It is an excellent indicator of when you should shift gears. It can tell you when you are wasting gas, if the idle is too high, or if the carburetor is set for too rich a mixture. It can detect a host of engine problems, from a sticking valve to a compression or manifold leak. It is invaluable as an engine problem detector because it spots the problem in its early stage, giving you a chance to remedy it before it can cause serious damage. This can save costly repairs later. It is like having your finger on the pulse of your engine. Look at Figure 21 to see how a vacuum gauge reacts under some of the conditions it can

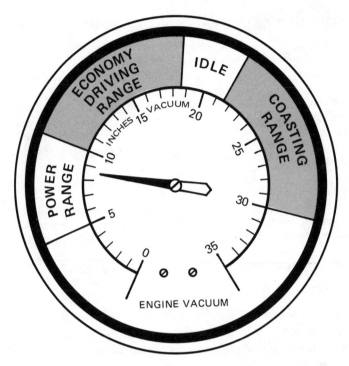

Figure 20. A typical vacuum gauge.

detect. Having this information visually available in the driver's compartment is like having a master mechanic sitting beside you at all times. The vacuum gauge—don't leave the garage without it!

◇ ◇ ◇

By itself or in combination with a vacuum gauge, a tachometer is another valuable aftermarket device for your car. Popular with performance buffs, it can also be an aid to everyday driving. A tachometer is a device that measures the rpm's (revolutions per minute) of your engine at any given moment. It tells you exactly how fast the engine is running. With a tachometer mounted on the dash you *know* your

CONDITION OF ENGINE	POSITION OF GAUGE POINTER
Good condition	Steady around 18
Needs carburetor adjustment	Fluctuates between 10 and 20
Burnt valves	Steady at 18 with periodic drops to 10
Weak valve springs	Up and down between 10 and 25
Worn valve guides	Fluctuates between 15 and 20
Sticky valves	Same as for burnt valves but pointer drop is less pronounced
Bad valve timing	Steady in the range between 10 and 15
Ignition timing needs adjustment	Steady at 15
Leak in head gasket	Fluctuates between 7 and 20
Manifold air leaks	Steady low reading around 12
Obstructed muffler or exhaust	Pointer drops from normal to 0

Figure 21. Some conditions a vacuum gauge can detect.

idle speed is set correctly and you *know* the proper intervals to shift for top economy and engine performance. It can be valuable during the break-in period of a new or rebuilt engine, when it may be desirable to limit most of the driving to engine speeds under 2,500 rpm's. Although it is not a "must" item like the vacuum gauge, it is nevertheless a desirable addition to any car.

Oil pressure, ammeter, and engine temperature gauges are covered in the section on driving habits.

New-Car Options

When purchasing a new car, one item to be very choosy about is the rear axle ratio. Most buyers aren't aware that they have a choice and they end up buying the car "as is." What is the rear axle ratio and how can it affect car life? The U.S. Department of Transportation defines the axle ratio as "the ratio of the revolutions of the drive shaft (transaxle for front wheel drive) to the revolutions of the wheel. . . . Generally, a low ratio, such as 2.53, means less engine wear and better fuel economy than a higher ratio, such as 3.55." In other words, with a low axle ratio it takes fewer revolutions of the drive shaft to make the wheels turn one complete revolution. In the first example above, the drive shaft would have to turn around 2.53 times for the wheels to go around once; with the higher ratio, the drive shaft would have to turn 3.55 times to accomplish one revolution of the wheels. Obviously it will take less engine work to turn the drive shaft 2.53 times compared to 3.55 times, but in each case an equal distance is traversed by the car. This is the reason you get better economy and extended engine life with a *lower* rear axle ratio. Buy a car with a low axle ratio and essentially you will be purchasing thousands of free extra miles for the car.

When you put pressure or strain on your muscles (as in weight lifting), they respond by becoming stronger and more resilient. Unfortunately your car doesn't react in the same way—if it did, the car would never wear out. The car reacts to pressure and strain by wearing out at those spots that are continually afflicted.

An excellent way to combat this wear is to invest in an overdrive unit. Overdrive will save fuel and will reduce engine wear. It acts as another higher gear, allowing the engine to loaf by reducing the rpm's necessary to keep the car moving. Although most overdrive units are not really effective until the car reaches or approximates highway cruising speeds, they are nevertheless a viable engine- and fuel-saving option. If highway driving is your forte, they are even more valuable.

Aftermarket or add-on overdrive units are now available, and although rather expensive to purchase and have installed, they may be worthwhile if you have decided that this is "the" car.

◇ ◇ ◇

New car companies are now also offering overdrive units in automatic transmissions. Automatic overdrives will give the same fuel-conserving and engine-saving benefits as the ones with a standard transmission.

Five-speed standard transmissions are becoming more common day by day. The fifth or highest gear acts in much the same way as an overdrive unit and should be treated as such. Most likely, manufacturers will recommend not engaging the fifth gear until the car has reached the 40- to 45-mph range, much the same as an overdrive. Five-gear transmissions are a good investment if used properly.

A note of caution: Many owners of five speeds have a tendency to use the fifth gear at speeds below the recommended level, if for no other reason than because it is there. Overdrives or fifth gears should only be engaged when the car has reached the designated speed. Using these units at lower speeds is false economy, as you could cause engine damage by lugging in too high a gear.

For an average driver, cruise control can save some gas at highway speeds. If you do a lot of highway driving, it is a worthwhile investment because it saves gas and relieves the tedium of the foot on the accelerator. It has minimal value as an engine extender, being of some value only in that it keeps the car at a constant speed. By staying at one speed you don't have to constantly feed gas to build speed back up, or back off to let the car slow down. Since highway driving under good conditions is the easiest type of driving on your car, it will be hard to justify cruise control as an engine-saving addition. Buy cruise control for economy and driving pleasure only.

Did you know that built-in engine heaters are offered as options on many new cars? You learned of their value in Chapter 5, and they are an extremely wise option choice if offered. Check with your new-car dealer to see if they are available for the new car you are considering.

A U.S. Department of Transportation report says that "diesel engines can provide as much as 25% increase in fuel economy compared to the same size gasoline engine." Diesels are attractive because of their fuel-extending characteristics. They last a lot longer, too, than their gasoline-fed counterparts. Given the same care and consideration as a comparable gas engine, the diesel will wear longer, sometimes by a wide margin. Diesels are an excellent choice if you are considering a new car and are interested in economy and long life.

Leftovers

Any add-on device that promises more miles per gallon or longer engine life and works by the extra air principle should be avoided. Extra air, especially unfiltered air, sucked into the engine over a long period of time can do more harm than good.

You might want to check out some of the companies offering cylinder deactivation conversions. They work in much the same way as the Cadillac 8-6-4 system. The idea is good in theory: If you don't need the power of all eight or six cylinders, why use it? For instance, under cruise conditions an eight-cylinder engine might deactivate four cylinders because it only needs four to keep it cruising. Essentially you are turning off the cylinders you don't need. As a gas-saving and wear-saving investment they bear investigation.

You probably never think of a locking gas cap as a wear preventive item, but it could be. It might save you from losing a tankful of gas or getting a handful of dirt in the tank.

While you're at it, a hood lock will serve a similar purpose. It prevents another type of hood from raising yours, helping himself to the battery, and leaving as his calling card a handful of dirt thrown down your oil filler pipe.

LPG, LNG, and Dual Fuel Conversion Systems

Take a close look at Figures 22 and 23. They show the intake manifold fuel mixture quality under cold-start and normal engine operating conditions, using different types of carburetors. As you can see, most

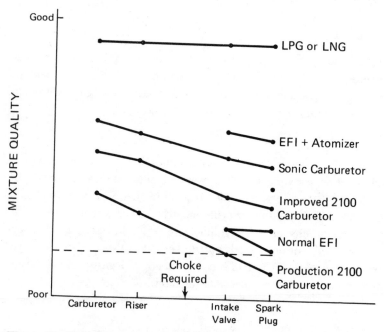

Figure 22. Ford Motor Company estimate of induction system mixture quality trends under cold-start and drive conditions (LPG = liquefied petroleum gas; LNG = liquefied natural gas).

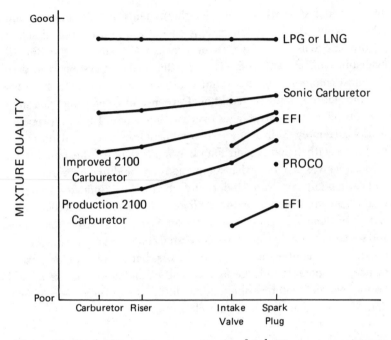

Figure 23. Ford Motor Company estimate of induction system mixture quality trends under hot operating conditions.

mixture qualities lie somewhere in the middle ground between poor and good. Under cold-start conditions all lean heavily toward the poor side. Now look at the top line in both charts. It rates "good" across the board, obviously superior to the carburetors depicted directly below. These are the mixture qualities exhibited by liquefied petroleum gas—propane (LPG) or liquefied natural gas (LNG). These graphs speak very highly of the quality of both these fuels.

There are numerous companies across the nation now offering conversions from regular gasoline engines to ones using LPG or LNG. Interest in and use of these systems to date has been limited mainly to fleet owners and an occasional adventurous individual. Also available are dual fuel systems, which offer the benefits of both gasoline and LPG driving. Dual fuel conversions enable you to use either gasoline or propane with just the flick of a switch. Because of the limited availability of propane or LNG fuels, the dual fuel system is to date the most common. For the owner who really wants the most from his car and doesn't mind the additional expense of converting, dual fuel systems offer many advantages over gasoline alone. LP-Gas (propane) works extremely well in internal combustion engines, and no major problems with it have been found. Among some of the benefits an owner receives are that exhaust emissions are held to a bare minimum and carbon gum and varnish deposits are virtually eliminated from the engine, meaning longer engine life (engine life of around 200,000 miles is *not uncommon* for vehicles in *fleet* use). Spark plugs last much longer and so does the oil, because fuel-generated contaminants are nil. Fewer repairs, less maintenance, lower fuel costs, better cold-engine performance, comparable mileage figures, and extended engine life all add up to a winning combination. Although this is an expensive modification, it is one that deserves your closest scrutiny.

Tires—Just Between You and the Road

Although tires are definitely not an "option," they are something every car owner must purchase sooner or later. And by buying the right kind of tire for your car and your kind of driving and climate, you will help extend the overall life of the entire car, engine included. So, loosely translated, tires qualify under the heading of engine- and car-saving add-ons.

If you are in the market for a new set of tires you won't want to make a move before you have a copy of the U.S. Department of Transportation's *Uniform Tire Quality Grading* guide in your hands. In my opinion, it's one of the best things Uncle Sam has ever published, and the even better news is that it's FREE. This comparison guide lists every passenger car tire sold in the United States with the exception of snow tires, space-saver or temporary use spares, or tires with nominal rim diameters of twelve inches or less. Each tire is individually graded in three areas: treadwear, traction and temperature.

The following is quoted from the guide:

The treadwear grade is a comparative rating based on the wear rate of the tire when tested under controlled conditions on a specified government course. For example, a tire graded 150 would wear one and a half ($1\frac{1}{2}$) times as well on the government course as a tire graded 100. The relative performance of tires depends upon the actual conditions of their use, however, and may depart significantly from the norm due to variations in driving habits, service practices and differences in road characteristics and climate.

The traction grades from highest to lowest are A, B, and C, and they represent the tire's ability to stop on wet pavement as measured under controlled conditions on specified government test surfaces of asphalt and concrete. A tire marked C may have poor traction performance. The traction grade assigned to this tire is based on braking straight ahead traction tests and does not include cornering or turning traction.

The temperature grades are A (the highest), B, and C, representing the tire's resistance to the generation of heat and its ability to dissipate heat when tested under controlled conditions on a specified indoor laboratory test wheel. Sustained high temperature can cause the material of the tire to degenerate and reduce tire life, and excessive temperature can lead to sudden tire failure.

The grade C corresponds to a level of performance which all passenger tires must meet under the Federal Motor Vehicle Safety Standard No. 109. Grades B and A represent the higher levels of performance on the laboratory test wheel than the minimum required by law.

The temperature grades are established for tires that are properly inflated and not overloaded. Excessive speed, underinflation, or excessive loading, either separately or in combination, can cause heat build-up and possibly tire failure.

Remember, these grade designations are required by government regulations and must be stamped on each and every tire. They are designed to be used for comparative purposes only.

Purchase a good tire pressure gauge and a tread depth gauge. These two items can do more to promote overall tire life—and overall engine and car life—than perhaps any other items mentioned in this chapter. And the best part is that they cost so little. A pair of these gauges can be purchased for less than five dollars. (For instructions on how best to use a tread depth gauge, see Chapter 8.)

8

Adjustments, Inspections, and Services That Prolong Car Life

Although this book was written for the car owner who enjoys doing some of his or her own servicing and repair work, it is also aimed at the vast majority of owners who are dependent on a repair shop to keep their cars going. Even if you do some of your own work, you no doubt find it necessary to engage the help of an experienced mechanic or technician at times. Finding a good, competent, and honest repair shop, one with trained technicians and modern equipment, is absolutely imperative if you desire a car that performs well and has a chance of living a long life. A shop that recommends preventive maintenance measures is one with your car's best interests at heart; one that "gets to know" a car is an owner's first-line defense against unnecessary wear and repairs. Finding a good repair shop isn't easy, but it is well worth your time and effort if you have a car that you want to last.

Mechanical Adjustments

Cars with mechanical valves (adjustable) should be serviced in accordance with the manufacturer's schedule. Valves that are out of adjustment and whose tolerances are incorrect can overheat, cause preignition, and contribute to premature engine failure. Close attention must be paid to this adjustment, especially if the engine is air cooled.

If you still have an automatic choke, don't forget to have it adjusted for both summer and winter driving. Summer will require a less rich setting and the choke should be set accordingly. A hand choke, highly recommended here, will save you this adjustment.

Want to be guaranteed maximum spark output at the spark plugs? Each time they are serviced the edges of the electrodes should be filed to a nice clean, sharp edge. Look at the electrode of a new plug to see exactly how it should look. Electrical charge tends to congregate more along sharp edges than on rounded surfaces. For this reason the plug will have more fire if the electrodes are sharp.

The ignition system must have its correct polarity if the plugs are to receive maximum voltage. Reversed polarity, usually caused by an inept mechanic's switching the primary wires at the coil, can seriously diminish available voltage and can cause plug damage if left uncorrected. Make sure polarity is correct, especially after having a battery, coil, or distributor replaced.

If you are a backyard mechanic and you like to do your own tune-ups, more power to you (no pun intended). However, a word of caution is necessary about setting ignition timing by ear or, as it is sometimes called, power tuning. *DON'T DO IT!* Ignition timing is too fine an adjustment to be set reliably by ear. Setting the timing to where a slight ping or rattling is heard upon sudden acceleration can be a dangerous engine-defeating habit. Many variables such as gasoline octane, outside air temperature, humidity, and how good your ears are can throw even the best-trained expert off the mark. What may seem good today may be a disaster tomorrow. Best and safest advice: Use a timing light and set to manufacturer's specs. Then, if you wish to advance timing slightly due to climatic or engine fuel variations, do so a degree at a time, testing the car after each setting.

One of the most important and often overlooked adjustments (even master mechanics are guilty of this sometimes) is the *one-way* relationship between timing and dwell. This relationship is very critical if top engine performance, mileage, and life are desired. Unfortunately, many mechanics and hosts of weekend knucklebusters aren't even aware such a relationship exists. When setting either timing or dwell (adjusting the distributor points), remember that when you change the dwell you also change the timing. If you set the timing, however, the dwell doesn't change. *Always set the dwell angle first, then set the timing.*

Too many tune-ups are done where the timing is set first and then the dwell. This has the effect of completely changing the timing again and makes the original setting, no matter how accurate, worthless. If you are having your car tuned at the local garage, it might pay to mention this to the mechanic—but do it in a nice way.

If you advance the ignition timing to take advantage of a higher octane gasoline or perhaps alcohol injection, remember that an over-advanced ignition can cause combustion chamber temperatures to soar. Over a prolonged period this additional heat can spell disaster for the engine. Be prudent when advancing the ignition; do it only a degree at a time. In no case should it be advanced over five degrees total.

Let's turn our attention now to one of the most critical adjustments on any car—the air/fuel ratio. Recall that the richer the fuel mixture, the better the chance of engine deposits' occurring. The air/fuel ratio is simply the amount of air that is burned in relation to one part of fuel. For absolute engine efficiency it is one of the premier adjustments on your car. What, then, is the proper air/fuel ratio?

You can conscientiously follow every suggestion in this book, but if the carburetor air/fuel ratio is too rich, your efforts won't be totally rewarded. The air/fuel ratio must be set "on the lean side" to obtain best mileage. It may be the single most important adjustment you can make to improve gas mileage and it is critical to have it checked and any necessary changes made. The best and most economical way to do this is to take your car to a garage that has an exhaust gas analyzer. This machine will "read" your car's exhaust and tell you if the air/fuel ratio is correct or needs changing. If the ratio is too rich, the garage will probably suggest changing either jets or metering rods to bring it into a more economical range. Some overrich carburetors, when leaned-out, will improve economy up to 5 mpg! Make sure you don't over-lean (an air/fuel ratio of 15 : 1 is usually excellent), because you can damage valves and spark plugs and get erratic engine performance if the carburetor is starved.

A glance at Figure 24 will verify that the best setting is somewhere around 15 parts air to 1 part fuel (15 : 1), that is, "on the lean side" for maximum efficiency and reduced emissions. Recall that anything we do to improve gas mileage will also have a positive effect on engine life and performance. This is an excellent example.

Services and Inspections

DON'T CLEAN IT—CHANGE IT! Remember these five words the next time you think of cleaning the air filter element. It is better not to try to clean the *paper* air filter element; instead, replace it with a new one. Most paper elements are usually cleaned by tapping them on the ground to shake out the dirt or by blowing them with an air hose from the inside out. You can do more harm than good by at-

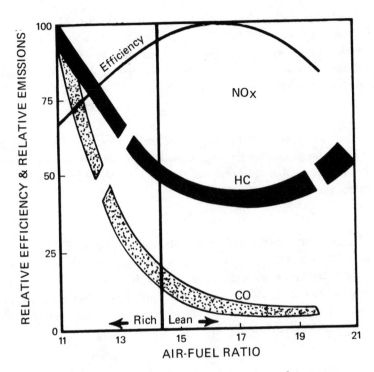

Figure 24. Effect of air/fuel ratio on efficiency and emissions.

tempting to clean the element this way, because once the filter is put back in place and the engine is started up, particles of dirt that were lodged in the element and consequently loosened by the tapping or air blowing are sucked into the engine. We have seen what abrasive grit can do to an engine; in fact, abrasive wear is the most common cause of engine failure. To help prevent it, don't attempt to clean the air filter element. An air filter element is relatively inexpensive and is cheap insurance against the ravages of dirt and grit. (This advice doesn't apply, of course, if you have an oil-bath or an oil-soaked air cleaner element.)

◊ ◊ ◊

Be certain the air cleaner *cover* is screwed down tight. If not, un-filtered air can circulate over the top of the filter element and be drawn into the engine. There also should be a gasket between the carburetor and the air cleaner. A loose fit at this point will allow uncleaned air to pass—a gasket ensures a snug fit.

When changing air filter elements, make sure you also clean the inside of the air cleaner housing. Usually a considerable amount of dirt becomes trapped on the bottom of the pan. This should be wiped clean before a new element is put in.

There is one way that you can get extra use out of an air filter element, providing it is not too dirty. Without attempting to clean it, simply rotate it 180° from its original position in the housing. This puts the cleanest area of the filter next to the bulk of the incoming air and rotates the most soiled area 180° away. However, if there is any doubt about the cleanliness of the filter, always change it.

Never run your car for any length of time without an air filter. A lot of drivers do this, thinking they will get better mileage from the unrestricted air flow. Not really. All you are doing is writing yourself a ticket for an early engine overhaul.

Don't purchase any paper air filter element that claims to be a lifetime product. There is no such animal. What you should be looking for mainly is an element that can remove particles ranging in size from 10 to 35 microns. These are the particle sizes that do most of the damage in an engine. Most proprietary filters today can remove this size dirt, some just do it better than others. Buy the best quality air filter you can find.

◇ ◇ ◇

Oil-bath or oil-soaked filters should be cleaned and reoiled frequently. If dust is encountered in your driving, clean the filters immediately after the vehicle is put away. These types of filters should be serviced no less than at every oil change and preferably twice between oil changes.

◇ ◇ ◇

The above advice applies to paper elements also—if a dust storm or similar conditions are encountered, change the filter at the first opportunity.

◇ ◇ ◇

The heat riser or manifold heat control valve is a simple butterfly valve located at some point in the exhaust manifold. It functions in much the same way as the radiator thermostat. This thermostatically controlled valve is important because when the engine is cold it remains closed, forcing exhaust gases to one side of the manifold. This helps the engine warm faster. When the engine warms, the valve opens and allows exit of hot exhaust gases through both sides of the exhaust manifold. If this valve becomes stuck open it will prolong engine warm-up; if stuck closed, the engine will tend to overheat. Stuck in either position it can cause erratic engine performance, in particular, rough idling. A stuck valve can also shorten engine life. Be certain this valve is serviced periodically. A few drops of solvent (don't use oil) on the hinges at every oil change or lubrication should do the job. It should move freely up and down when finger pressure is applied.

◇ ◇ ◇

Nothing will damage an engine faster than a clogged or restricted tailpipe, muffler, or catalytic converter. Any restrictions in the entire exhaust system should be removed and major dents straightened. An engineer was puzzled because his car had suddenly lost power and would hardly run. Investigation of the engine showed nothing, and it remained a mystery until his son asked him what the mud was doing in his exhaust pipe. Mud removed—problem solved.

One of the *must* items to service on any car is the PCV or Positive Crankcase Ventilation system. It must be clean and the PCV valve must work freely. A clogged PCV system, as simple as it is, can lead to rapid oil contamination and a deposit-fouled engine. Gas mileage also suffers. Replace or clean the PCV valve as required.

Don't forget the EGR or Exhaust Gas Recirculation valve. If this valve malfunctions or becomes stuck, it can have a very negative effect on fuel economy and the engine. Be certain it is checked and its proper operation verified each time the car is tuned.

Underinflated tires wear faster and you have to replace them sooner. That's not very good economy. Underinflated tires also mean the engine has to work a lot harder to move the car because of the increased rolling friction generated by the soft tires. Keep tires inflated to the *tire manufacturer's* recommended pressure or even a pound or two higher. Don't use the owner's manual or car manufacturer's suggested pressures because they are usually lower so the car will have a nice soft ride. Try this experiment: If you own a bicycle, check that the tires are at normal pressure and take it out for a ride. Now remove about 10 pounds of air from the tires and take it over the same route. See the big difference underinflation can make on the amount of pedal energy you must supply to move the bicycle? It takes a lot more energy, and you burn a lot more calories pumping the bike on underinflated tires. Do you think you could last longer pedaling the bike with the soft tires or the hard ones? Your car, really, is no different.

Regular use of a tire pressure gauge—I recommend checking tire pressure at least once every two weeks—will do more to ease the burden on your tires and engine than practically any other device. But don't forget the tread depth gauge. It can also help extend the life of your tires. Here's a method I have used over the years that works.

Check your tires about once a month with a tread depth gauge and keep a running log of your readings. Take three measurements on each tire: one at the left edge, one in the center, and one at the right edge. Insert the tread depth gauge (calibrated in 32nd's of an inch) and note the readings. Your log will look something like this for each tire: left = 7/32, center = 8/32, right = 7/32.

These three readings taken across the width of the tire tell you whether or not the tire is wearing evenly. If the readings begin to favor one side—for instance, 7/32, 7/32, 5/32—you know that the tire is wearing too much on that side. Frequent tread depth readings give you a chance to catch any tire wear patterns before they can permanently damage the tire. You can take the necessary action (add or remove air from tires, have tires balanced or wheels aligned, replace shock absorbers, do necessary front end work, etc.) before the condition worsens. This saves your tires and makes your car safer and more economical to drive.

Automobiles heavily laden with emissions-control equipment literally carry performance robbers with them. Emissions-control devices have become a necessary evil and we have had to learn to live with them. The best an owner can do is to keep them clean and in perfect working order. Even the best-intentioned tampering can do more harm than good. In an Environmental Protection Agency test, private garage mechanics were asked to alter emissions controls to get better mileage and performance. The results? EPA said that "emission control system tampering is more likely to hurt fuel economy than to improve it. Such tampering virtually always makes emissions worse, and *can cause deterioration in engine durability.* Regular maintenance according to manufacturer specifications improves both emissions and fuel economy." (Emphasis mine.) In other words, tampering with emissions-control systems can cause your engine to wear out faster, cut fuel economy, *and* add pollutants to the air.

The highest quality oil, used in a mechanically perfect engine, will fail miserably if attention is not paid to the basic maintenance routines of servicing the carburetor and emissions-control systems.

Keeping the outside of the engine clean is important, too, as it can affect the way the car performs. Dirty, grease-layered engines can "seal in" heat and force the engine to run hotter than it should. Dirt and grease also tend to disrupt electrical flow in ignition wiring and/or battery cables and can cause hard starting. A clean engine on the outside helps guarantee that no dirt will accidentally find its way inside. And, too, doesn't a nice, clean, new-looking engine make you feel better?

On older cars make certain the draft tube, located under the car at the oil pan, is free of any obstructions and has not been damaged to the point it cannot vent properly. On many older cars this draft tube and the oil breather cap are the only means of ventilating the crankcase.

A clogged crankcase ventilation system, particularly in winter, can cause deposit buildup, which will block oil pump screens and oil passages and hinder lubrication of the entire engine. Cold weather and city-type driving with little or no crankcase ventilation will speed buildup of oil and water emulsions, which, when combined with the unburnt products of the fuel (cheap, bargain-type fuels add to this problem), form an unyielding sludge. Even the best quality oil and fuel can't go one-on-one with a clogged crankcase ventilation system.

◇ ◇ ◇

Always replace the PCV and EGR (Exhaust Gas Recirculation) valves as per recommendations. Never attempt just to clean them at the change interval. Do as the man says—replace them.

If you have a battery that has caps for water fill, use only distilled water when you replenish the cells. This prevents possible mineral buildup inside the battery and will help ensure that a full charge is always available.

For the same reason, you might consider using distilled water in the radiator also; mixed with one of the fine proprietary rust- and leakproof coolants available today, it will provide the best in radiator protection and guard against mineral precipitation inside the radiator. This can be really helpful in areas where hard water is the rule.

Most machine shops have available a water-miscible oil that can be added to the radiator. A few ounces mixed with the coolant ensure long troublefree radiator and water-pump life. It also gives extra protection against rust. In lieu of this, auto supply stores and service stations carry a water-pump lubricant that will do the same job. It's a good idea to add one or the other to your radiator.

Check the front of the radiator directly behind the grill and remove any accumulation of bugs and dirt. A friend was having overheating problems and was stumped as to the cause until he spotted a large paper bag that had lodged itself in front of the radiator. Bag removed—problem solved. Keep the radiator clean inside and out to ensure proper engine performance at proper temperature.

Just because the antifreeze/coolant you are now using is designated as "permanent" doesn't really mean that it is. Even "permanent" type antifreeze can wear out, become contaminated, and lose its effectiveness. Antifreeze/coolant should be changed and the cooling system flushed and cleaned every twelve months or as the owner's manual recommends.

Too many automobile owners think about their automobile cooling systems only when the weatherman forecasts the first freeze of approaching winter. Even the name of the coolant—"antifreeze"—makes you think of cold temperatures. Antifreeze was initially developed specifically to prevent the water in your cooling system from freezing during the winter.

Today, antifreeze/coolants do much more. The best antifreeze/coolants are formulations of the highest quality ethylene glycol that contain foam, rust, and corrosion inhibitors to provide year-round cooling-system protection. Have you ever wondered why you see cars pulled over to the shoulder of the road with their hoods open, steam erupting from the radiators, during the hot summer stop-and-go traffic in our congested cities? Most of these cars have air conditioning, power brakes, power steering, power this and power that! These conditions represent the most severe service possible for adequate cooling of your engine. Overheating can be a frustrating, but often preventable, problem.

The two major ways to help prevent overheating of your cooling system are: (1) Be sure you have the proper amount (and mixture) of antifreeze/coolant in your cooling system, and (2) Do not neglect proper cooling system maintenance.

When you think of antifreeze/coolant, do not limit your thinking to cold-temperature protection. Modern automobile engines, with all of their extra equipment, operate at very high temperatures and require high-temperature cooling system protection as well.

For optimum high-temperature protection, your cooling system should contain a 50/50 mixture of water and antifreeze/coolant. Water, of course, boils at 212°F; a 50/50 mixture of water and antifreeze/coolant boils at 226°F. This is a 14-degree margin of safety—it could make a difference! Now, to complicate things just a little, modern cooling systems operate under pressure (14–15 pounds per square inch). Under this amount of pressure, water boils at 246°F; under this same amount of pressure, a 50/50 mixture of water and quality antifreeze/coolant boils at 262°F. Therefore, in a properly maintained cooling system under 15 pounds per square inch of pressure, your protection is extended to 262°F. The recommended 50/50 mixture also provides optimum rust and corrosion protection.

You might think that if a 50/50 mixture of antifreeze and water is good, then 100 percent antifreeze must be great. This is not true. Concentrations over a certain amount will reduce the effectiveness of the antifreeze. Pennzoil, for instance, does not recommend concentrations greater than two parts antifreeze to one part water. Pure antifreeze will freeze between 0°F and −4°F. As odd as it may sound, it's the addition of water that gives it fluidity and a low-temperature freezing point.

On the flip side, pure antifreeze-coolant is only about 50 percent effective in removing heat from an engine compared to a proper mixture of antifreeze and water. That's important in hot summer driving. In addition, the performance additives (silicates, nitrates, rust inhibitors) in antifreeze also require water to be properly suspended and effective.

The second major cause of overheating is lack of proper maintenance. Antifreeze is a lot like motor oil: It needs to be changed periodically. For optimum protection, change your antifreeze once a year. The radiator cap is also very important. It acts to seal the cooling system and allows it to operate under pressure. If the radiator cap malfunctions or is not closed securely, your cooling system is much more likely to boil over. With a 50/50 mixture of antifreeze and water and a faulty radiator cap, your boil-over temperature reduces to 226°F, down from the 262°F optimum.

Even a high-quality antifreeze/coolant will not perform satisfactorily unless the cooling system is properly maintained. According to a U.S.

Department of Transportation study, problems with the cooling system are the No. 1 cause of mechanical breakdown on the road. Cooling system neglect is what causes those problems. Keep your cooling system in top condition and you won't add to that statistic.

Your owner's manual should give you the correct maintenance schedule but here are some general guidelines:

1. Check existing coolant concentration.
2. Test thermostat to insure proper functioning.
3. Inspect hoses and water-pump drive belts.
4. Test pressure cap and inspect radiator filler neck.
5. Pressure test for leaks.
6. Monitor coolant level and change if dirty or rusty.

Opening just the radiator drain cock will remove only about half of the used water/antifreeze from the cooling system. Commercial kits are available for proper flushing of the cooling system that allow a water hose to be connected to the heater inlet hose, forcing the used solution from the heater coils and engine block through the inlet of the radiator. If the used solution is dirty or rusty, an alkaline flush-type cleaner will help remove sludge and loosely held rust.

After filling the cooling system with the correct concentration of quality antifreeze/coolant and water, run the engine with the heater setting on "high" until the normal driving temperature is reached. This releases any trapped air and insures a proper mixture. If your car is equipped with a plastic reservoir, it should be filled to the correct level with the same mixture of antifreeze and water.

Using the proper concentration of antifreeze/coolant, along with proper maintenance procedures, will eliminate most cooling system problems. On extremely hot days (95–105°F), in heavy stop-and-go traffic, one other tip might get you home safely: Roll your windows down and shut off the air conditioner until you can resume freeway speeds.

◊ ◊ ◊

Remember that the amount of additive content in the coolant varies from manufacturer to manufacturer, with the cheaper brands containing less. Bargain brands may also contain less glycol—the main ingredient that protects against boiling and freezing—and more water than name brands. Quality antifreeze/coolant is made with approximately 97 percent glycol. An expert for an antifreeze maker tells me that some bargain brands may contain as little as 50 percent glycol. So be careful—you get what you pay for. Cheap antifreezes may not give the protection necessary to keep your car operating efficiently.

All openings should have caps or covers that fit snugly. Gas cap, oil filter and/or breather cap, radiator cap, oil and transmission dipsticks, power steering reservoir covers, and the like should all be either pushed in or screwed on tight. These areas are susceptible to water and dirt infiltration. Tight-fitting covers with good seals guarantee that the engine is operating in an environment closed against unwelcome outside elements.

Incidentally, a locking gas cap is good insurance against another type of outside element—the local neighborhood gas thief.

With the heavy emphasis placed on gas mileage in the past few years, you are probably well aware by now that any weight you can pare from your car will contribute to better mileage. What you may not be aware of is that it can be beneficial to car life also. Obviously the engine won't have to work as hard when extra weight is removed from the car. We're not advocating chopping off fenders or removing bumpers, but taking those cement blocks and snow tires from the trunk will help. If you don't think weight is important, ask yourself this question: Which do you think would last longer if driven continually, a one-ton pickup with an empty bed or a one-ton pickup with a full one-ton load?

The Most Important Inspection
You Can Make

Intake manifold leaks caused by any of the following can upset the air/fuel ratio and result in rough idling and poor economy: loose manifold connections or leaks occurring in intake manifold vacuum lines or at the carburetor flange; loose manifold nuts; distortion or misalignment of gasket surfaces at the intake manifold and carburetor-attaching flange; damaged or improperly installed gaskets; a leak at the juncture of the carburetor and the throttle rod where the rod may have worked loose the vacuum seal. To demonstrate the importance of a sealed intake manifold (no leaks), McDonnell Douglas Corp. was able to improve the fuel mileage of some new automobiles with these problems by as much as four miles a gallon simply by resurfacing and properly matting the carburetor to the intake manifold! As you can see, air leaks into the intake manifold can be costly.

A large leak, such as a vacuum hose that has become disconnected, may make itself known by a loud hissing sound or can be detected by visual inspection. Less obvious leaks can be located by squirting a little gasoline or household oil in and around suspected areas while the engine is idling. If there is a leak, the gas will be drawn through it and into the engine, where it will cause an increase in engine speed as it is burned along with the regular fuel. Don't forget to also check hoses to vacuum-operated units such as the windshield-wiper motor, windshield washer, and distributor advance.

Figure 25 shows how air can infiltrate between the carburetor and manifold. This is one area that should be checked and rechecked for proper gasket alignment and tight seal. Manifold leaks can cause fuel mixtures to become disrupted, leading to rough engine performance; they can also cause serious engine wear conditions. In his book *Tuning for Performance*, Bill Carroll gives a dramatic example of what can

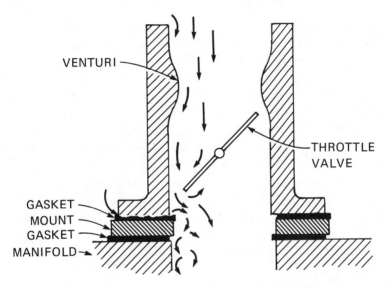

Figure 25. Air leaks at the carburetor-intake manifold juncture.

happen to an engine if even the smallest intake manifold leak is left unattended. A relatively new engine that was not performing properly was torn down; the combustion areas were found to be loaded with melted sand. Upon closer inspection, engineers found a small hole in the intake manifold. The car's owner, driving under dusty conditions and unaware of the small hole that was drawing dust and grit into his engine, wore out the engine in a few thousand miles. The mechanics who tore it down noted that it looked like it had been driven a few hundred thousand miles. Don't let manifold leaks go unchecked; find them and fix them.

Tune, Lube, and Change

Have the car lubricated at least as often as prescribed in the owner's manual. If possible, stay with the car while it is being serviced. Become familiar with the lubrication points and make sure the attendant reaches each and every one of them (your owner's manual will show you the points that should receive regular attention). A garage that wipes the grease fittings clean before lubing or replaces missing ones is a garage that deserves your return business. As the car is being greased or the oil changed, check underneath it if the garage allows. This is an excellent time to look for signs of fluid leaks: oil, transmission fluid (especially at the front and rear seals), brake fluid, rear axle lubricant, radiator coolant, shock absorber fluid, and power steering fluid. Any exhaust-system damage can easily be seen and wheels can be spun to listen for dragging brakes or a defective wheel bearing. This is also a good time to inspect the tires for any possible damage or unusual wear patterns. It would normally cost you extra to take the car in and have it put on the rack to make these visual inspections, so why not do it while the car is already being serviced and save the extra lift charge?

Although most of us have been taught about changing the oil, very few have made it a habit to change the other lubricants and fluids. It's easy to rationalize away these prescribed services. The car is running just fine and it really doesn't seem necessary to change the rear axle lubricant or the coolant or the transmission fluid. Why disturb a sleeping dog? Because that dog may get up and bite you later on if you don't wake it and feed it now. Preventive maintenance is a prime key to long troublefree car service. Granted, it may be hard to drag yourself down to the garage on a Saturday morning or to make an appointment at the dealership—and it is even harder when everything seems to be working so well—but that's just the point. We want to keep it that way. Changing fluids on or before schedule is the best insurance these usually trouble- and maintenance-free units will continue to give good service.

Although gear lubricants are not subjected to the combustion-based contamination experienced by engine oils, it must be remembered that, particularly during the "running-in" period, small particles of metal are constantly being removed from the gear teeth, synchronizing clutches, and other mating surfaces. Much of this debris settles to the bottom of the gear casing, but in course of time the amount actually circulating with the oil becomes sufficient to cause damage, particularly to the ball or roller bearings incorporated in the unit. The periodic changing of the lubricant should therefore be carried out in accordance with manufacturers' recommendations, the oil being drained with the unit at near working temperature. It is particularly important to change extreme-pressure oils at the specified intervals; such lubricants have only a limited life and eventually lose their extreme-pressure properties, with the result that the film strength reverts to that of the original oil. Additionally, corrosive elements can appear after extended periods of use.

Something almost every car owner is guilty of ignoring is the rear axle of the car. Sure, the lubricant level is checked each time the car is greased (at least it should be), but when was the last time the rear axle lubricant was changed? Indeed, has it ever been changed? From the above we see that it should be.

In colder climates or in cars used under severe service conditions, cut the manufacturer's change intervals by 20 to 30 percent for long axle life. A magnetic rear axle drain plug is also recommended.

Axle or differential lubricants, like oil, can differ in weight. When changing, select a weight commensurate with the type of climatic conditions the car is most likely to experience. A warm-weather car might do best with an SAE 80W-90 or an SAE 85W-90, while a cold-weather car would be most efficient with an SAE 75W.

Transmission fluid and rear axle lubricants should only be changed after they have reached operating temperature and are in their most fluid state.

It is amazing that automatic transmissions last as long as they do and function, as a rule, so flawlessly. Other than the rear axle, the transmission wins the prize for being the most overlooked and yet dependable mechanism on the car. Have you ever changed the automatic transmission fluid? Fresh fluid at prescribed intervals and an occasional band adjustment are all an automatic transmission asks for. Average transmission life can easily be doubled by just following these simple rules. If the car is being used mostly under severe service conditions, the drain and change intervals should be shortened considerably; 20 to 30 percent should be lopped off the recommended severe service recommendations. This is not asking much for years of troublefree, dependable service.

◊ ◊ ◊

Long Transmission Life

Automatic transmission fluids are probably the most complex of all automotive lubricants, including even the most sophisticated, synthetic motor oils. They can be made from as many as 15 elements, whereas a typical motor oil may contain only 7. According to an article in *Automotive Engineering* magazine, transmission fluids are subjected to severe oxidation and a number of other conditions that can lead to ". . . deposits of sludge and varnish in the transmission, . . . an increase in corrosion of copper-alloy bearings, . . . hardening of various elastomeric (rubberlike) seals, and . . . glazing, flaking and wear of clutch plates and bands."

Any one of these conditions is bad news for your transmission and wallet, but all can be avoided by changing transmission fluid before oxidation can alter its protective characteristics. The big question is how to know when that time has arrived.

The change interval given in your owner's manual will do just fine for most transmissions in most areas of the country. If you want to be more precise, just use the time-proven blotter test:

Place a drop or two of transmission fluid from your car (you can get the drops by removing the transmission dipstick) on a clean piece of white blotter paper. If you can't find blotter paper, a paper kitchen towel will work just fine. Next to this drop, place another one or two drops, of equal size, of fresh, unused transmission fluid. (If you don't have a can of it handy, a service station will probably give you a few drops.) Wait one hour, then observe the spots on the paper.

The fresh-fluid spot is your reference point. It will be large and have a reddish or light-brown color. Compare your transmission fluid's spot to the one made by the fresh fluid. Is it about as large as the fresh-fluid spot, and does it have some red or light-brown coloration? Or is it small and dark?

Automatic transmission fluid that does not exhibit good spreadability and coloration is probably suffering from oxidation and should be replaced. A spot that approximates the color and size of the fresh fluid indicates that the fluid is still fine and should be left in the transmission.

This fairly foolproof test is easy to perform and should be done about every two months. As soon as you notice the fluid spot getting smaller, darker, and more concentrated, you will know it is near time to get the old stuff out and the fresh stuff in.

The blotter test is a simple, inexpensive way of keeping that complicated, expensive automatic transmission troublefree for a long, long time.

If you have a standard transmission, this doesn't mean you can ignore it. The oil must be changed here as per schedule also, although it is not as critical as in an automatic. Learning to shift properly, along with periodic transmission oil changes, are all that is necessary to get maximum life from the unit.

It is very helpful if both the automatic and standard transmission drain plugs are magnetic. The metal filings created by the meshing of gear teeth are one of the major causes of wear in these units. Magnetic plugs keep these wear-producing particles out of circulation where they can do no harm.

Be certain the type of automatic transmission fluid you use is the one meant for your car. For instance, General Motors and Ford Motor Company use different types of fluid, and although one may work in the other's cars, it can't do the exact job the original fluid can. Transmission fluid is a highly refined blend of additives; what is specified for a GM car won't give top performance in a Ford product, and vice versa.

Although there are some exceptions to the rule—Ford recommends Type F automatic transmission fluid for its cars' power steering units —use transmission fluids in transmissions and power steering fluids in power steering units. Transmission fluids contain a "seal sweller" additive that can negatively affect the rubber parts in power steering units. Power steering fluids don't contain these swellers. Unless your owner's manual designates otherwise, follow the above advice.

A word about packing the front wheel bearings: Never *add* grease; always clean the bearings and repack them with *fresh* grease. Make certain it is a high-quality EP (extreme-pressure) multipurpose grease. The moly- or graphite-fortified EP greases or partially synthetic greases are excellent choices.

In normally wet climates or during periods of heavy rain in normally dry climates, extra-frequent lubrication should be the rule. Water on the road will wash lubricant away, leaving the fittings exposed to water infiltration and rusting. Metal-to-metal contact and consequent wear are more common under rainy conditions.

Remember to follow the owner's manual recommendations for the other important services such as cleaning emissions-control systems, changing gasoline filters, and the like. The mileage/time relationship applies here also, and these areas should be serviced at X number of days or X number of miles, whichever comes first.

Work done by Shell Research Limited and others shows that engine-tuning factors have a major influence on fuel economy and that correct mixture strength settings and conformity with motor manufacturers' ignition specifications are particularly important. The major maintenance factors affecting fuel economy appear in the following order of decreasing importance.

(a) Idling mixture strength and engine idling speed.

(b) Basic ignition timing/dwell angle.

(c) Vacuumatic ignition advance.

(d) Centrifugal ignition advance.

(e) Spark plug condition.

This shows how proper engine tune can affect fuel economy. If you substitute the words "engine wear" for "fuel economy," the statement will be just as accurate. Idle mixture strength can be a major factor in engine wear and oil contamination. The others also play important roles.

"Caution must be exercised so that the steps taken to improve fuel economy by modifying the lubricant do not have a deleterious effect on other operating factors such as oil consumption, engine cleanliness or wear protection." Not only engine tune is important; the type of oil also plays a starring role in preventing engine wear.

◇ ◇ ◇

How often, then, should the car be tuned? Barring any outstanding problems, at least as often as prescribed by the manufacturer. However, this should be a guide only; you should learn to tune up within the time or mileage framework specified. The interval should never be longer than that prescribed by the manufacturer; it may need to be shorter for a number of reasons, including the type of driving done. Heavy city driving, cold weather conditions—in essence, the same conditions that dictate an early oil change—mean a shorter tune-up interval. An excellent aid in determining the proper tune-up time is to watch and keep accurate records of your gas mileage. Any significant variation for two consecutive fill-ups probably indicates the car is in need of a tune. As a rough rule, the tune-up deterioration should be slow and the gas mileage drop will also be slow. Any consistent drop of 10 percent below the average mileage should be a sign that the engine needs attention. If you have a vacuum gauge, an overall drop in engine vacuum for the time it takes to use a tank of gas is another good indicator. A slowly blackening tailpipe (when it is usually a nice gray color) is also an indication. Erratic engine performance detected by you, the driver, means that you have already passed the time when a tune-up should have been performed.

Would a car owner be more likely to have his car tuned if, as he grinds and grinds the engine on a cold winter morning, we used the expression "He's wearing down his engine" instead of the more common "He's wearing down his battery"?

The condition of the ignition system is the most important factor in starting your car in cold weather. When other engine components are not properly maintained, even a new or well-charged battery can be worn down quickly before the engine starts. This is because the voltage required to start a car increases when the engine has such maladies as broken or cracked ignition cables, worn spark plugs, or a worn or corroded distributor cap or rotor.

Problems are compounded during wet or cold weather, when the components require even more current to perform basic operations. Electricity, like water, seeks the easiest path along which to flow. Faulty wiring or ignition components interrupt or drain the flow of an already diminished electrical supply. For example, worn spark plugs require easily twice the current new ones do. Cold temperatures also affect the capacity of the battery to produce necessary starting power. At 80°F a battery has its maximum capacity. This drops to 60 percent at 32°F and 46 percent at 0°F. Often during cold or wet weather the battery may not have enough power to start the engine, but it may not be the battery's fault.

Tests by Champion Spark Plug Company demonstrated the relationship between these voltage-required and voltage-available factors. Two cars were purchased as-is from used-car lots. One, a Chevrolet, had a conventional ignition system; the other, a Dodge, had electronic ignition. Both cars were able to start in warm-weather conditions. They were then "soaked" in zero-degree cold with the following results:

The Dodge did not start in four 3-second attempts. A new battery was installed, but another attempt at starting was unsuccessful. Technicians then tuned the car, adding new spark plugs and distributor components and resetting the timing to factory specifications. Using the original battery, five new attempts averaged starts in 2.67 seconds.

On the Chevy, with the battery and engine still in as-is condition, there was one unsuccessful start, one start after 9.52 seconds, and one start at 2.31 seconds. When a new battery was installed, the average starting time was 9.87 seconds in eight attempts. With new spark plugs and the original battery, the average starting time was 1.67 seconds. With the engine tuned and still using the old battery, starting time averaged 1.75 seconds. According to Champion, these test results should negate the long-held assumption that the battery is the cause of most of the trouble when starting a car in cold weather. A new battery could not help start these cars at 0°F, yet once the engines were tuned even the old battery could provide sufficient voltage to fire the engine.

The conclusion wasn't surprising: A prewinter tune-up is indispensable for dependable starting. I couldn't agree more. And remember, a tuned car, winter or summer, is a car that is going to last longer.

9

Easy Checks That Help Determine "How the Engine Is Doing"

The Tailpipe

Want to know at a glance how your engine is doing without even raising the hood or lifting a tool? Walk to the back of your car or truck and look at the inside of your exhaust pipe. What do you see there? Rub your finger around the inside and see if the deposit is wet. Is it oily? Is it dry? The color and condition of the deposit on the inside of the tailpipe are two of the best indicators of engine shape. Just as an automobile traveling over fresh snow will leave tire tracks, so, too, will an engine leave its imprint on the tailpipe. By looking at those tire tracks in the snow, you can get a pretty fair idea of the condition of the tires; by the same token, looking at the imprint the engine leaves on the exhaust pipe gives you an idea of the condition of that engine.

Ideally, the inside of your tailpipe should be dry, and the deposit should be a fine, light, flaky powder. Its color should range anywhere in the light gray to light brown range. Any deviation from these conditions means the engine is not tuned properly or is showing signs of oil consumption and wear. Incidentally, this is one of the first things you should look at when buying a used car.

A wet, black sooty tailpipe (with no appreciable trace of oil) probably indicates a too-rich carburetor mix or a stuck or improperly adjusted automatic choke, both conditions detrimental to engine wear. A black oily deposit could mean that the engine is using oil, which may be the fault of worn piston rings or other major components. It could also indicate less severe problems, but for our purpose it is showing us that something is wrong somewhere, and if this is a car you are considering buying, tread cautiously. A white glazed look to the inside of the exhaust may be an indication that the engine is running too hot or the timing is too far advanced. If not corrected, these conditions can quickly damage an engine.

So if you want a pretty good indicator of engine (and carburetor) condition, take that short trip to the back of your vehicle, bend down, and peek inside your tailpipe. Don't be afraid to get your finger dirty. Run it around the inside of the pipe. (Make sure the engine is turned off and has cooled down, because a hot tailpipe can burn.) Besides being a check on internal engine conditions, the tailpipe can give information about the carburetor or fuel injection system, the type of fuel being used, and the heat range of the spark plugs.

The Valve Covers

Another easy way of getting some idea of what's going on inside the engine is by removing the valve cover or covers. This is a simple operation and usually entails only the undoing of four bolts or screws on each cover. Removing the valve cover will show you, at a glance, the condition of the entire rocker arm assembly. If it and the inside of the valve covers are clean and no sludge or particle buildup is present, then you can rest assured that your driving habits and oil-change intervals are just about right. If they are dirty and sludge-contaminated, then you know something is wrong and should take appropriate action to remedy it. A valve cover check each time the spark plugs are removed is a wise practice and will help you spot and correct trouble before it has a chance to do much damage.

The Windows of Your Engine

Wouldn't it be great if engines had little windows placed in critical wear areas that could tell us at a glance how things were at those points? Unfortunately, engines don't have windows, but they do have a number of small openings where you can check on the internal condition of the unit. One of the most economical methods of determining engine condition (you can do it for free yourself) is spark plug analysis or reading. For the home mechanic, removing and studying the spark plugs is a simple, effective way of "glancing into the engine." Each plug, by its condition, reflects what is going on inside its individual cylinder. What is happening to the spark plugs, then, is what is happening inside the combustion chamber.

Before we get too far into "plug reading," here are two initial procedures that should be followed closely. If you are removing the plugs yourself, first clean the area around each plug and blow the dust or dirt out of the plug socket. The small cans of compressed air available at automotive stores are ideal for this. Keep in mind that just a grain or two of sand that finds its way into the cylinder can cause damage. Upon removing the plugs, make a note of which plug came out of what hole. It doesn't do any good to read a plug and then forget which cylinder it came from. Mark each plug with masking tape and a number as it is removed, or place the plugs in numbered containers. Experienced mechanics should also follow these procedures, and if you are present while someone else is doing the work, don't be afraid to remind him or her of it.

Looking at the plugs and understanding what you are seeing and what can be done to correct the situation (if need be) is an art. This is why a good mechanic is invaluable. Even if you take the plugs out yourself, you can still carry them to a garage for analysis. A good spark plug reader can spot many engine conditions and write a prescription for their cure. Among maladies that can be detected and corrected are incorrect spark plug heat range (too hot or too cold for your type of driving), worn piston rings or valve guides, deposits from the use of inferior quality fuels, melted sand (silica) deposits indicating a faulty air or fuel filtration system or leaks in the intake manifold (this can be a harbinger of sudden engine demise due to the severe abrasive action of sand and grit particles that can be sucked in through the leaks), engine running too hot or too cold (indicating cooling system malfunction), over-advanced ignition timing, faulty carburetion (either too rich or too lean), stuck heat riser valve, clogged EGR or PCV valve, clogged air cleaner or oil breather cap, and literally a host of other ailments. These are some of the more common ailments that can be spotted by a knowledgeable spark plug analyst. You can see just how valuable a service it can be. Unfortunately, detailed spark plug reading is beyond the scope of this book. It is our purpose here to familiarize the reader with the process and the tremendous amount of information it can furnish about an engine. Every engine, when the plugs are removed, is trying to tell a story, even if it is nothing more than that everything is just fine —which is exactly what we want to hear anyway.

If you would like to become acquainted firsthand with the plug-reading fundamentals, there are a number of excellent books on the subject. In addition, spark plug companies are more than happy to send you information on plug analysis with explanations of what caused the state of the plugs being studied. This can be extremely helpful to the beginning plug reader and in many cases will be all that is needed to accurately diagnose your engine's condition and learn what, if any, remedies can be applied. Perhaps all you may need is a set of plugs one heat range higher, or maybe an over-rich carburetor is the cause of the dark wet plugs, which in turn are causing that low speed miss. Correcting these problems as they are uncovered can save you costly repairs later and will ensure future troublefree driving.

Emissions Inspection Reports

Save those vehicle emissions inspection reports; they are valuable longevity aids. Compare the figures from one year to the next. You don't have to be an automotive engineer or a mathematician to do it.

A consistent drop or holding pattern in emissions numbers from year to year indicates that you are following maintenance and driving practices that will help extend the life of the vehicle.

High or erratic emissions results, even if they are within the "pass" range, can be early warning signals that something is amiss and should be corrected if you want the car to last. And the sooner it's corrected, the better.

Emissions can be reduced through conscientious maintenance and consistently good driving habits and low emissions mean a more efficient and longer-lasting vehicle. Being a number watcher will help you achieve that goal.

10

Break It In Right

Those First Miles Can Be the Most Important

The wear process that takes place inside an engine or transmission is, on the whole, not very desirable, but it can be useful in one circumstance. In a new engine, accelerated wear takes place during the break-in period. This wear is actually beneficial and plays a large part in determining how the engine will run and how long it will last. The initial accelerated wear process, if implemented properly by the driver, sets the stage for the slow, almost nonexistent wear stage that should follow. Close attention to the break-in techniques described in this section will help ensure that your new car lasts and performs well.

◇ ◇ ◇

The most critical time for a new-car owner is the break-in period. It is here, during the first few thousand miles of driving, that the pattern for future engine and transmission life is established. Just as instilling good health habits in a child will pay lifetime dividends, so will being diligent with the new car break-in. Proper break-in means a payback of many extra years' service from your automobile.

Most new-car manufacturers recommend a special type of driving for the first few hundred miles and then a moderate driving regimen for the next five hundred or so miles. The initial few hundred are the most crucial. A conscientious owner, adhering strictly to the break-in recommendations during those critical miles, will do more for the car at that time than any other single practice.

Modern engines demand different break-in techniques from those your father used; gone are the laborious miles spent at a snail's pace. In fact, today's cars require very little deviation from what you would normally be doing behind the wheel. Modern break-in recommendations are very simple: Drive moderately for the first few hundred miles. After the first one hundred miles, legal speed limit driving is desirable. Also recommended are brief accelerations while the car is at cruising speed. In some manuals that is the entire new car break-in routine. Although we have no argument with the above recommendations, they do not go far enough. More and closer attention should be paid to this crucial time, for in those first five hundred miles or so you are drawing a blueprint for future car life and performance.

What then, is the best technique to adopt during the running-in period? In the first place, the number of cold starts should be kept to a minimum, and the initial four or five hundred miles is far better covered in two or three longer journeys than in a period of short runs made locally. When the engine *must* be started from cold, minimum use of the choke is helpful, and the running temperature should be reached as soon as possible. This is best achieved by getting under way as soon as the engine is running, keeping the vehicle in an intermediate gear, the speed low, and a very small throttle opening until running temperature is reached. The aim should be to run the engine under a minimum load with engine revolutions in the neighbourhood of 1,500–2,000 rpm. In cold weather particularly, a radiator blind, adjustable from the driver's seat, is an asset.

With the engine up to running temperature, driving can proceed more normally. The speed in top gear should be limited to about 40 miles per hour, but the overriding requirement is that the engine must not be allowed to labor, nor should the engine speed be allowed to fall too low. Conditions which call for more than half throttle should be met by changing down into a lower gear, the road speed being adjusted so that the engine speed does not exceed about 2,500 rpm. It is of vital importance to avoid maximum load; it is far better to have too high an engine revolution speed than to allow the engine to labor at a lower speed with excessive throttle opening. A new engine must not be allowed to idle longer than is absolutely necessary for, although the bearing loads are very small, other lubrication conditions will be at their worst and the running temperature will quickly fall. Indeed, it is prudent, and convenient, to set the idling speed of a new engine rather high. As running-in proceeds and frictional values fall, the idling speed will progressively increase and probably require adjustment.

The preceding recommendations fit comfortably within the simple framework of most new car break-in rules. As you can see, there is more to it than just driving moderately for the first few hundred miles. It would also be very beneficial if the car could be kept in a garage (preferably a heated one) during the break-in period and if some type of engine heater or radiator heater were used to lessen the cold start wear penalties. "The initial four or five hundred miles is far better covered in two or three longer journeys than in a period of short runs made locally." This is very important. The break-in period, after the first fifty to one hundred miles, is an ideal time to take that trip you have been planning. Vary your highway speeds and never stay too long at one constant speed.

One thing recommended for today's engines that was considered disaster just a decade or so ago is brief accelerations while the car is moving. While you are driving on a secondary road or a freeway frontage road, try to maintain speeds in the 30 to 40 mph range, then do this: Push the accelerator to the floor and hold it there until the car reaches the speed limit; at that point ease off the gas gradually. Occasional accelerations of this kind are beneficial, and along with the practice of varying speeds will help seat the piston rings to the cylinder walls and ensure a tight engine. (New cars have small grooves cut into the cylinder walls that act as canals for the oil to flow through and reach the important boundary areas. The above process helps wear off these grooves properly and lets the piston better match the conformity of the cylinder walls.)

During the first few hundred miles of engine operation the high-spots are removed in part by plastic deformation and in part by local pressure welding and subsequent shearing. Sufficient heat is generated during the latter process to increase the running temperature of the bearing to such an extent that the viscosity of the oil is reduced. This adds to the frequency with which the contacts are formed. Provided the bearing surfaces are relatively lightly loaded and the oil supply is copious, this latter process is not severe and the bearing surfaces eventually settle down and gain their normal working surface. If the bearing surfaces are subjected to high loads and associated high temperatures during the running-in period, the wear rate will be very high and scuffing or seizing of bearing surfaces may well result.

The bearing clearances of the new engine are minimal so that the cooling flow of lubricating oil is also less than normal. The high initial frictional losses not only lead to increased running temperatures but also increase the power output required of the engine.

The driving techniques and general operational conditions during the running-in period should be designed to combine minimum bearing loading with optimum lubrication conditions.

Working within the framework of the owner's manual, the above techniques will ensure you are doing all that is possible to break in the new car properly. "It is of course important that the initial oil change and general servicing are carried out strictly in accordance with the manufacturers' recommendations. During this period, the amount of wear debris finding its way into the lubricating oil of both engine and transmission is abnormally high."

There is another point where we differ from the owner's manual—the initial oil change. Most manufacturers now recommend that the initial oil be left in and changed at the regularly prescribed interval, for instance, when the car reaches 7,500 miles or 12 months, whichever comes first. We believe this is a dangerous practice. For absolute protection the oil should be changed after the first thousand miles. Period. We have seen that the amount of wear debris in both the engine oil and transmission fluid is very high during the break-in, and the one real assurance you have that it won't be doing any harm is to get it out. The initial transmission fluid change should also be shortened considerably for the same reason.

If your car contains a *special break-in oil* (see owner's manual), never change that oil before the break-in interval is up. These oils are specially formulated and contain special additive packages that assist the process of breaking in. (Note: Although most new cars today do *not* contain a special break-in oil—most manufacturers now use a high-quality commercial brand oil—if yours happens to be one of those that does, be sure to leave it in for the entire specified period.)

Many new-car dealers have available an engine oil supplement especially formulated to assist the regular oil during the break-in process. A new-car owner would be wise to use one of these break-in supplements, for they usually contain extra anti-scuff and EP (extreme-pressure) additives, which can be valuable in helping the engine wear itself in properly. These extra additives will help metal conform to metal, allowing mating parts to become very close in conformity to each other. These break-in supplements are also good when used in a newly rebuilt engine.

When breaking in a new car, it is a good idea not to run the air conditioner for the first one or two hundred miles.

You won't find this in any owner's manual, but rest your car for an hour or so after each couple of hours of continual break-in driving.

In the same vein as the above, engineering studies have shown that hot starting problems can be fairly common in new engines when they are restarted shortly after high-temperature operations. In other words, if you have just used your new car for a long highway run or if you have been using it in the city with the air conditioner on, let it sit a while before attempting to restart it. This is good advice for older cars, too.

We have seen that occasional full-throttle accelerations while the car is moving can be beneficial to the break-in process. Full-throttle accelerations from a dead stop, however, should never be attempted.

As mentioned in the break-in procedure, never drive for long periods of time at one constant speed. Vary your speed up and down—don't stay with one speed for more than a few minutes. To help with this practice, ease up completely on the accelerator every so often and let the car slow down a bit. This creates more engine vacuum, which can assist in getting more oil into the upper cylinder area where it is most needed.

◇ ◇ ◇

Earlier we said that you could buy two identical cars from the factory and one could outperform the other, give better economy, and last longer due to variances in factory tolerances. If you are lucky you may just get that "perfect car." On the other hand, you may end up with the proverbial lemon. Lemons, like that perfect car, are realities too. If you have been saddled with a car that just isn't right from the start and your dealer or area representative is unable or unwilling to help, then your best bet is to go to the top man in the company. The following list is provided as lemon-aid for the harassed new-car owner. You can't get a car to last forever if you get a lemon to start with. Hopefully, by writing one of the persons on the list you can get your problem satisfactorily resolved. The following are the addresses of the heads of the major automobile companies.

The Lemon Complaint List

Chairman of the Board
Chrysler Corporation
P.O. Box 1919
Detroit, MI 48288

President
Ford Motor Company
The American Road
Dearborn, MI 48121

President
General Motors Corporation
General Motors Building
Detroit Building
Detroit, MI 48202

Vice-President
Porsche Audi Division
Volkswagen of America, Inc.
818 Sylvan Ave.
Englewood Cliffs, NJ 07632

President
BMW of North America, Inc.
BMW Plaza
Montvale, NJ 07645

President
Fiat Motors of North America,
    Inc.
155 Chestnut Ridge Road
Montvale, NJ 07645

President
American Honda Motor
    Company, Inc.
100 West Alondra Blvd.
Gardena, CA 90247

President
Mazda Motors of America, Inc.
3040 East Ana Street
Compton, CA 90221

President
Mercedes-Benz North America,
    Inc.
1 Mercedes-Benz Drive
Montvale, NJ 07645

General Manager
Nissan (Datsun) Motor Company
    Limited
560 Sylvan Ave.
P.O. Box 1606
Englewood Cliffs, NJ 07632

President
Peugeot Motors of America, Inc.
1 Peugeot Plaza
Lyndhurst, NJ 07071

*Vice President and General
    Manager*
Renault USA Corporate Group
100 Sylvan Ave.
Englewood Cliffs, NJ 07632

President
Saab-Scania of America, Inc.
Saab Drive
P.O. Box 697
Orange, CT 06477

President
Subaru of America, Inc.
7040 Central Highway
Pennsauken, NJ 08109

President
Toyota Motor Sales—USA, Inc.
2055 West 190th Street
Torrance, CA 90509

President
Volkswagen of America, Inc.
27621 Parkview Blvd.
Warren, MI 48092

President
Volvo of America Corp.
1 Volvo Drive
Rockleigh, NJ 07647

11

Caring for the Interior and Exterior

Although the main emphasis in this book is on preserving the major mechanical components of your car, the condition of the interior and the exterior are probably of equal importance when it comes time to trade the old buggy in. More important, a car that looks and feels good encourages the owner to keep up its other parts.

Paints and Finishes

In the past few years, some manufacturers have departed from tradition in the way they paint their new cars. They now use a base-coat/clear-coat finish. General Motors, with many of its new cars, is a prominent member of this new fraternity.

The customary method is to use a layer or layers of pre-pigmented enamel or lacquer paint. The base-coat/clear-coat method uses at least two layers, but each is different. The first, or base, layer gives the car its color. The finish, or clear, coat is then applied over the base coat; it is usually some type of clear acrylic polymer, a variation of the clear stuff you put on your kitchen floor. Many carmakers believe the clear coat gives the finish more luster and a deeper, mirrorlike look.

There is another reason for clear coating: The clear acrylic polymer seals the pigment layer from the elements, thus making it less susceptible to deterioration and oxidation. With ordinary paint, the pigment is exposed to sun, wind, and water, but clear coat protects and seals the pigment and acts like a good wax job on an enamel- or lacquer-finished car.

Here are some tips, courtesy of GM, on how to care for a car with a clear-coat finish. As you will see, they aren't too different from those on washing and waxing enamel or lacquer finishes.

• Care must be taken not to scratch the surface. Clear coats tend to haze up and get a cloudy look when scratched. Use a gentle car-wash soap. Hose off any grit and grime before applying a sponge or cloth to the finish. The more dirt you can remove before you apply hand pressure, the better. When you begin washing the car, be certain to rinse the sponge or cloth often. If you take your car to a commercial car wash, make sure it has soft brushes.

Although base-coat/clear-coat finishes don't need waxing as frequently as other types (once or twice a year is suggested by GM), a number of precautions are in order.

• Don't use any type of power polishing unit. I test-drive new cars daily, and many of these brand-new cars bear the scars of the most dastardly paint torture device ever invented by man: the electric polisher. The finishes are covered with swirl marks—prima facie evidence of an electric rotation polisher. Clear coat or not, don't use them.

• Use a mild, non-abrasive cleaning wax/polish. Always apply the polish by hand. If your car has aluminum mag wheels, check with your dealer to see if they are protected by a clear-coat finish. Many are. If so, do not—and so many of us do—use a brush to scrub them. This will scratch the clear coat and give the wheels a fuzzy look instead of the brilliance you desire. This is a little-known fact that should be tucked away in your automotive memory bank.

• Nicks and chips in a clear-coat finish are treated a bit differently from those in enamel or lacquer paints. In the latter, a touchup paint of the same color is used to dab on the spot. With clear coat, the pigment must be applied first, then the clear coat. Kits containing both are available at auto parts stores.

As with any type of paint, clear coat requires that you make some occasional effort to protect and enhance its beauty. I hope the above tips will help your finish live a long and beautiful life.

Although many of the suggestions given for clear-coat finishes also apply to pigmented enamel or lacquer finishes, extra care must be taken to protect these vulnerable paints from sunlight, acid rain, smelter smoke, bug smears, bird droppings, and other environmental and road hazards. Probably the best protection available is a couple of coats of one of the better polymer waxes. The suggestions above should be followed before and while applying the wax.

If the paint shows signs of dullness or oxidation, take the advice of the Chemical Specialties Manufacturing Association, a Washington, D.C.-based group, and treat the finish with a mild polishing compound (usually white in color) before applying the polymer wax. If the finish is badly oxidized, a stronger rubbing compound (orange in color and more abrasive than the white polishing compound) may be necessary.

After the car has been washed, dried, and, if necessary, treated with a polishing or rubbing compound, apply the polymer wax according to instructions. Never apply it to a hot surface, and always wax the car in the shade. Once the wax has been applied, don't use any type of soap or cleaner on it.

If you live in the Sunbelt, you might look for a polymer wax that contains ultraviolet absorbers (UVAs). These additives will minimize the sun's oxidation effect on the finish and keep the paint from fading and chalking.

Always remove bird droppings from your car's finish as soon as possible. They contain acids and strong dyes and can etch themselves into your finish if left unchallenged. You don't have to wash the entire car; just remove the droppings with a wet towel or sponge before they harden. Newly painted cars are particularly susceptible because the paint hasn't had sufficient time to dry and harden.

If you choose a light-colored car for your next purchase, its body finish will last longer and stay more lustrous through the years. Light colors are much less susceptible to oxidation from the sun's rays and the paint won't deteriorate nearly as fast. Light colors are especially good choices in the Sunbelt states, where they help in keeping the car interior cool.

Park in the shade instead of the direct sunlight when given the choice. You'll save the paint and interior fabric (especially the dash) from the ravages of the sun's heat. Cracked dashes, rotted upholstery, and blistered paint are the common results of prolonged parking in the sun.

Never use a laundry-type detergent when washing your car. The strong detergent action will dull the finish and wash away any protective coating now on the car. Use one of the milder soaps specifically formulated for automobile exteriors. A check of any auto supply store will uncover a number of satisfactory brands.

Invest a few dollars in a can or bottle of matching touchup paint for your car. After a period of nominal use, any car will start to accumulate road badges or chips in the paint. Touch up these chipped spots periodically with matching paint to keep the car looking good and to fend off water and salt from penetrating to the bare metal where they could cause rust. Before using the touchup paint, be sure to wash the chipped areas thoroughly with mild soap and water, rinse, and let dry completely.

◊ ◊ ◊

While on the subject of the car's lustrous finish, never wipe dust off your car with a dry cloth. Remember how dust and dirt can harm the inside of an engine? They will do an even better job on your paint, leaving scratch and swirl marks as evidence of your overambitious cleaning. Always rinse with water first and then wipe with a wet cloth. If you can't wet wipe it, don't wipe it at all.

Vinyl Roofs

All vinyls contain plasticizers, liquid ingredients added by the manufacturer to give the vinyl flexibility. As these plasticizers are lost through evaporation and chemical reactions started by heat, the vinyl becomes brittle, the backing between the vinyl and the roof starts to separate, and cracks begin to appear. Variations in temperature accelerate the deterioration, and the vinyl starts to crack along its seams.

When a product that contains silicone (Armor All, for instance) is put on a vinyl roof, it does a number of things: The silicone additives lubricate the vinyl, while other ingredients impede the progress of cracks and blisters; ultraviolet absorbers protect against sun damage, while still other additives resist attack from ozone, which will cause vinyl to oxidize. Another inhibitor prevents the formation of fungus, mildew, and mold.

Many people think that using paste wax on a vinyl roof is good, but the wax, usually made by combining silicone, water, mild abrasives, and a hydrocarbon-based solvent, may have long-term deleterious effects: The solvent tends to remove the plasticizers from the vinyl and the abrasives may begin to chew up the stitching.

Vinyl Dash and Upholstery

Caring for vinyl interior parts—especially a vinyl dash—is a lot different from caring for a vinyl roof. Although direct rays from the sun help speed up its aging, a vinyl dash's main enemy is heat, which attacks the interface between the vinyl and foam backing (usually urethane foam). As plasticizers escape, the vinyl eventually blisters and begins to crack.

Vinyl upholstery on the seats and door panels is not affected as much by sun and heat and consequently will last longer. However, it should also be protected with preservatives each time the dash is treated.

It's important to note that any product meant to help protect and preserve vinyl or rubber won't stop the aging process. All vinyl and rubbers parts will eventually meet their maker, no matter what precautions you take, but regular application of preservatives will help delay the process and sometimes extend their life quite dramatically.

Before applying one of the commercial vinyl protectants and preservatives to your dash, you might consider this little trick. After the dash has been properly cleaned, apply a little sunscreen lotion to it. The higher the sun protection factor, the better. Just rub it in as you would on your skin. Then, after the sunscreen has had time to soak in, buff off any excess and apply the commercial protectant, which will help seal it in. I've found that this really helps, especially if you live in an area where dashes are subjected to a lot of strong sunlight.

When applying a dash cleaner or preservative, place a piece of cardboard against the windshield to avoid overspraying onto the glass. The chemicals in these solutions can adhere to the glass and form a hard-to-remove film.

By the same token, when you are cleaning the inside of the windows or windshield, lay a towel or some other protective cloth over the dash or the top of the door sills or rear windowsill. Glass cleaners contain harsh chemicals that aren't meant for use on plastics, vinyls, or interior cloth. Protecting one part while you are cleaning another will add life to both.

Car Covers and More

One of the best ways to insure that your car's exterior and interior are well protected is to invest in a car cover. Covers come in all shapes and sizes, so you won't have any problem finding one to fit your car.

A car cover is great protection against the elements. It will help keep the paint from fading and the interior from discoloring and cracking. It protects the interior from the direct rays of the sun and minimizes heat damage to the upholstery and dash. The best covers—which are also the most expensive—are made from 100 percent cotton, but any cover is better than none, especially if you park your car outside.

Make sure the cover is snugged down tight, because a flapping cover can rub paint from the car. For the same reason, don't transport your car with its cover on.

There are a number of companies that repair cracks and small nicks in windshields for a fraction of what it would cost for replacement. (Look in the yellow pages under the "auto glass" heading.) A resin is injected under pressure into the damaged area and fills in the cracks. When dry, the resin strengthens the glass and does a nice job of disguising the crack.

The sooner you repair cracks, the better, because contaminants will have less time to infiltrate the cracked area. The cleaner the cracks, the better the repair.

Do bumper stickers detract from the looks of your Drive-It-Forever beauty? Try spraying and soaking the stickers with some WD-40 or a similar lubricant or penetrating oil. Let it sit for a few hours and then try to scrape the stickers off.

You can also try using a blow dryer on them, but be careful—too much heat can damage some of those plastic or rubberized bumpers. It works best if the sticker is on a metallic surface.

Don't ignore the rubber parts of your car. There are a lot of them in the engine and on the body. At every oil change it's a good idea to rub a thin coat of rubber preservative over them. Silicone preservatives are readily available.

In lieu of the commercial preparations, an excellent substitute is hydraulic brake fluid. All rubber parts should be rubbed with one of these preservatives for ensured long life of hoses, and good tight-fitting seals around doors, hood, trunk, and windows. These preservatives will also help prevent cracking and rot, which are especially prevalent in hot climates.

◊ ◊ ◊

The main thrust of this book has been to show you how to make the engine, transmission, differential, and other major mechanical components of your car last. These are the car parts that can require major costly repairs, and they are the units that *must* function if the car is to be operational. As a rule, if you take care of the engine and other mechanical components, you will be diligent about caring for the body and interior. There are literally hundreds of excellent cleaners, solvents, soaps, waxes, and preservatives commercially available that will do a super job at cleaning upholstery, rugs, dashes, windows, mouldings, paint, chrome, aluminum, stainless steel, white sidewall tires, and so on. If you take a tour through a junkyard one thing will stand out—most cars don't look that bad and the main reason for their being there, besides those involved in collisions, was probably mechanical failure of one or more major components. Very seldom will you find a car on the scrap heap because of faded paint or a dirty interior. We feel that keeping the exterior and interior of the car clean and protected is a job almost anyone can do; it takes no particular expertise, just a lot of elbow grease. Keeping the engine, transmission, and other mechanical components functioning for a long time is the area most car owners need help with, thus this is where the emphasis has been placed in this book.

12

Other Ways to Prevent Automobile Senility

The Owner's Manual

New-car owner's manuals are probably one of the most ignored pieces of literature on the market today, and, sadly for the owner who ignores them, they are one of the most valuable. Most owner's manuals end up in the glove compartment where they are destined to spend the rest of their days amid the clutter of old cigarettes, road maps, and assorted coins. Occasionally they may be given a breath of fresh air when the owner wants to check warranty conditions or to see what that little button under the dash is for. More commonly it is pulled out to get at the flashlight. Very few owners use the manual for the purpose for which it was intended—to show how to get top performance from the car and make it last.

Who can know more about a car than the people who built it? Who can better know what should be done to a car, and when, than the manufacturer of that car? Not all manufacturers give the same recommendations, either—this is especially true when it comes to service recommendations for the engine because different design variations call for different service recommendations. The owner's manual is meant for your car alone. It is, in effect, a specific treatise designed and written for your make, model, and year car. Don't ignore your owner's manual; it's packed with valuable information and can be a very effective tool in your quest for automotive longevity.

Don't have an owner's manual? Most manufacturers are happy to send you one at a moderate fee. Check with a dealer that sells your make of car and ask to order one. This applies to older cars too, as most companies have manuals available for cars up to ten years old. Follow the advice in the owner's manual, along with the advice in this book, and you will be doing about everything possible to get the most miles from your car.

If you are unable to obtain an owner's manual for your present vehicle from a dealer or manufacturer, you can order one from Helm, Inc., P.O. Box 07130, Detroit, MI 48207. Give them the year, make, and model of your car, and they will send you an itemized order form. They also supply other out-of-date or hard-to-get manufacturer information sources, such as electrical system and shop service manuals.

Although there may be some truth to the old saw that most cars are not made to last, you can, by following the recommendations herein, make the phrase "built-in obsolescence" obsolete!

An invaluable aid to the car owner who does a lot of her or his own mechanical work, and a great adjunct to the owner's manual, is the manufacturer's service manual. This book has all the information necessary to assist you in performing even the most major of repairs. Most of them are profusely illustrated and show you, step by step, how to repair or replace just about any item on the car. Again, who should know better the easiest way to fix a car than the people who built it? Check with your dealer or look in your owner's manual for ordering information.

How to Store a Car

Many readers of my syndicated column have asked for the best way to store a car. Here is my reply, from my March 18, 1986, column:

A car is always better off stored indoors, preferably in a cool, dark, dry environment. Ideally, the temperature should never drop below freezing.

If you're going away for a few years, give the battery to a friend.

Drain the fuel system. Any gasoline left in the bottom of the tank should be sucked out with a siphon or other suction device.

After the tank is drained, the engine should be run until all the gas in the fuel lines, carburetor, fuel pump, injectors and other system parts is used up. If the car used leaded gas, run it with a gallon or so of unleaded before draining and drying the system. Unleaded gas left in the fuel system is less likely to form deposits when it evaporates.

Now the engine. Have the oil and filter changed as close as possible to the time of mothballing. Don't store a car with old oil in it. The contaminants in that nasty stuff will wreak havoc while you are gone.

Ideally, a can of molybdenum disulfide (MoS2) should be added when you change the oil. The car should run with the new oil and MoS2 for about two hours, if possible, before the final shutdown. The MoS2 will coat the engine parts and make them almost impervious to moisture.

Pull the spark plugs and pour about a teaspoon of fresh engine oil into each cylinder. Then replace the plugs. This will help coat the cylinders with protective oil.

All engine openings, particularly the air cleaner and the oil-breather cap, should be packed with absorbent cloth. The same applies to the exhaust pipe, but wait until it has cooled. Cotton towels will work.

With the exception of packing the exhaust pipe, these engine procedures should be done when the engine is warm. Otherwise, you will be sealing in moisture instead of keeping it out.

Release the tension on all the drive belts in the engine.

Top off the transmission and rear-axle fluids. If your automatic-transmission fluid hasn't been changed in the last 30,000 miles, it would be a good idea to replace it. Radiator coolant should not be drained.

The cooling system should be left wet to help preserve the various seals and gaskets inside. If the coolant is more than two years old, now would be a good time to replace it.

But here's an exception to the radiator rule: If any part of the engine is aluminum, drain the cooling system. The electrolysis set up by the aluminum and coolant combination can corrode and ruin an engine.

Brake systems should also be left wet. If the fluid is old, change it. Old brake fluid will corrode and pit metal brake-system parts if given enough time.

If the car will be in storage for a year or more, put it on blocks or jack stands. This takes the pressure off the wheel bearings, shock absorbers and other suspension parts. Remove the tires if they are in good condition. Leave them mounted on the wheels with the air pressure slightly reduced and store them on their side out of the sunlight.

If the car can't be put up on blocks, add another 10 to 15 pounds of air to the tires.

If the car is stored indoors, it is best left uncovered. If stored outside, a good quality car cover is recommended. A frame should hold it above the car's finish so it won't rub the paint. The car should be washed and waxed, and you should rub silicone preservative on all rubber door gaskets and other rubber parts. The interior should be cleaned and coated with a quality vinyl protectant.

If the car is stored outside, cover the dash, rear deck, and upholstery with clean white sheets or towels. Cover all the windows so the sunlight doesn't penetrate, but leave one of them open just a bit.

Keep a list of the things you have done and place it in the car. When you return, you'll know exactly what to do to get the car moving again (retighten belts, take out the engine packing, etc.).

Used Cars—Some Tips on Finding a Good One

If you are buying a used car directly from an owner, try to determine whether or not the car has been garaged or kept in a carport. This outside protection can mean a lot to the inside of an engine. All other conditions being equal, a garaged car will be superior to one left outside.

Ask to have a compression test done. If the owner has nothing to hide, there should be no objection. A compression test is a good means of determining the extent of cylinder wall and ring and piston wear, which in turn usually reflects the overall engine condition. The upper cylinder area is a boundary lubrication point and is hard to lubricate. If these areas show little or minimal wear—and a compression test will indicate to what extent they are worn—then most likely the rest of the engine is in good condition.

It's also a good idea to study the condition of the spark plugs at the same time the compression test is being run. Plug condition (see Chapter 9) is also an excellent indicator of what has been going on inside each individual cylinder. You're shelling out good money for that car, so don't be afraid to ask that these tests be permitted. If the owner objects, take your business elsewhere.

One of the best ways to determine the overall condition of an engine and its systems is to have it analyzed on a modern computer engine analyzer. Before running out and asking the first shop you come to to run a test, however, you should know that engine analyzers vary widely in their accuracy.

I recently wrote a report that studied and compared the three best-selling engine analyzers on the market today. The findings showed that one brand was far more accurate at diagnosing engine ills than the other two. This engine analyzer, the Allen Smart Engine Analyzer (SEA), uses expert system based technology and software. I would recommend going to a shop that has an Allen because, in my opinion, it has capabilities the others don't approach.

Be wary of the car that looks *too* good. Many of these too-shiny, too-clean cars have just come from the local detailing shop. There is nothing wrong with detailing a car, but it is better to see a car before it has been detailed to determine its *actual* condition. (Detailing is professional cleaning, washing, and waxing of the automobile interior, exterior, engine, and trunk.) A good detail shop can work wonders on the most dingy-looking vehicle, giving it an almost brand-new appearance. In the process of reviving the car, many telltale signs a prospective buyer should be aware of are glossed over. Steam cleaning and then painting an engine will temporarily hide oil leaks and make a worn-out chunk of iron look like it just came from Detroit. For my money, an "as is" car is better, for what you see is what you get. Then, after you are satisfied that the car is everything it is represented to be, you can have it detailed yourself if you so wish.

Another thing to remember when buying a used car: New car dealers usually keep the cream of the trade-in crop for their own used car lots; the remainder are wholesaled out to other used car dealers. You may pay a bit more for a used car from a new-car dealer, but chances are you will be getting a better car.

If you are considering buying a used car from a dealer, become familiar with the "Buyer's Guide" sticker that must be posted on every used car (for-sale-by-owner cars excluded) that explains how the car is being sold (as-is, with a warranty, etc.). It also contains much valuable information to help you determine which car is best for you and how to go about finding it.

The "Buyer's Guide" was originated by the Federal Trade Commission (FTC) as a consumer protection device, and an excellent one it is. Anyone in the market for a used car should read the FTC pamphlet that explains all about the "Buyer's Guide."

It can be ordered by sending 50 cents to:

Consumer Information Center–F
P.O. Box 100
Pueblo, CO 81002
(Request publication 44OT "Buying a Used Car")

I highly recommend it.

Tread carefully with a newly painted car. A little body putty and some fresh paint can convert a tired-out wreck into a new-appearing classic. Paint is also very effective in temporarily covering up rust, which will rear its ugly head after you buy the car.

Look twice—no, make that three or even four times—at a used car that has a trailer hitch before you buy it. Better yet, remember that trailer towing is severe service driving and don't buy it.

A friend of mind once bought a car that was just a bit over a year old and had 77,000 miles on it. It had been owned by an oil company service representative and had had good care, with all services performed at the prescribed intervals. Most of the mileage was highway driving. He said it was one of the best cars he ever owned.

Another acquaintance bought a car from the proverbial little old lady, who drove the car to the store or to the doctor's office and back. The car was eight years old and only had 19,000 miles on it. It was one of the worst cars the person ever bought. The point to be made here is: Don't let mileage alone influence you when buying a used car. The *kind* of miles is much more important than the amount.

Finally, a tip given me by a man who has sold cars for the past 30 years: When you are test-driving the car, turn the radio or tape player off. This experienced salesman tells me that turning the sound on while driving the car is the most common mistake buyers make. They are more interested in the quality of the sound system than in listening to the car. The stereo system masks other car sounds that a conscientious buyer should be listening for and creates a false sense of euphoria about the car. Listen to the stereo only after you have completely evaluated other areas of operation.

Rust—You Can't Drive It If the Body's Not There

Any car can rust. This car body and frame Enemy Number One has taken its toll on millions of automobiles. An all-too-common sight in many areas of the country is rusted and rotted cars, some running, some in their final resting places. The sad part is that many of these vehicles died prematurely, some perhaps just a few years old. You won't be able to "drive it forever," regardless of the mechanical condition, if the frame and body fall apart from rusting. The only good thing to say about rust is that it *can* be prevented.

In December 1975 the National Highway Traffic Safety Administration (NHTSA) published a Department of Transportation News Fact Sheet entitled "Automotive Rust—Its Causes and Prevention." Let's look at some of the recommended ways to prevent rust from literally eating up your investment.

Rust is the oxidation of metal exposed to moisture. In areas where corrosives and salts are used on the roads, the rusting and oxidation processes are greatly accelerated. This process can also be speeded up in seashore areas where the air is very salt-laden. Rust spares no part of your car but is especially prevalent in wheel wells, door rocker panels, and areas around body trim and moulding. It can also affect and eventually weaken the actual floor of the car and parts of the car frame.

A car ravaged by rust loses almost all of its resale value and—more important—is unsafe to drive or to ride in. It is not uncommon for exhaust to find its way into the passenger compartment through rusted-out parts of the floorboards. *Rust* is indeed a four-letter word. Let's look at some ways to eliminate it from our car vocabulary.

When you purchase a new car, make certain it has been *rustproofed* at the factory. Many new car dealers now offer guarantees against rust for a certain number of years—you can bet that every area of these cars prone to rust has been thoroughly rustproofed. If you buy a car without factory rustproofing, be sure to have it done immediately after purchase. Driving the car for even a few days may give rust the little edge it needs to get started. A quality, professional rustproofing will treat all rustprone areas, especially wheel wells, doors, rocker panels, and the like.

Rustproofing is not the same as undercoating. Many times these two are confused or used interchangeably. Rustproofing is a process that bonds some type of rust-preventive substance (a chemically effective primer or paintlike substance) to the involved parts. Undercoating is an asphalt-like substance that is sprayed over the rustprone areas. Undercoating is not as effective as a good rustproofing, but it is better than not having any protection. If the car is to be undercoated (undercoating is a good sound deadener), this should also be done at the factory or immediately after purchase. NHTSA recommends that the gas tank, exhaust system, and areas around the catalytic converter *not* be undercoated.

Since I wrote the original edition of this book back in 1983, car manufacturers have greatly improved the rust protection offered on new cars. And they have backed up their anti-rusting technology with blockbuster warranties. It isn't uncommon today to find new cars coming with five-, seven-, or even ten-year rust protection warranties. Many of these are even transferable to a second owner for a minimum fee. That's good news for the consumer living in the "rust belt" who is considering a new car. Is any of this new technology applicable to used cars? Is there something older-car owners should know that could help them in the battle against body rot?

After an hour of sloshing through salt-covered roadways, your car is covered with that all-too-familiar whitish film by which road salt betrays its presence. You are conscientious about the car and want to protect it, so you pull it directly into your garage, close the door, and feel good about having it out of the cold and snow. What you don't realize, however, is that you may have just contributed to the rusting process by putting your car into the exact environment needed for rust to begin its dirty work. I know that sounds crazy, but on a cold day in an unheated garage the inside temperature may be somewhere between 32 and 40°F. In this temperature range, conditions are just perfect for the chemical process that triggers rust. By treating our cars to winter shelter we may unknowingly be pushing them down the road to ruin.

If, on the other hand, the car were left outside where the temperature is most likely below freezing, no chemical reaction would take place and the rusting process would be put on hold. In this case it would have been better to leave the car outside—as far as rusting is concerned, anyway.

Similarly, when temperatures rise above 40 degrees, the salt solution begins to evaporate, and if the salt isn't in solution, that is, in liquid form, it can't do any damage. You can pour a whole sack of road salt on the hood of your car and as long as moisture doesn't get into it, it won't do any harm.

Between 32 and 40°F is the danger zone where the salt solution can chemically combine with metal to start or continue the rusting process. If possible, avoid storing your car for prolonged periods where temperatures are normally in that range. This is the time you want to be certain to wash the accumulated salts off the car as often as practical. If you don't feel like washing the car, a couple of bucks invested in the local car wash is a small price to pay for additional rust insurance.

A car wash is a good way to determine if the car has any body, window, or trunk leaks. Seal any leaks before the accumulated moisture can beckon rust.

A good way to check for leaks underneath the car is to spray the undercarriage with a powerful hose. After spraying (don't forget to spray the inside of the wheel wells), check under the floor mats and trunk mat for signs of moisture. Seal any cracks or holes with a permanent-type caulking compound.

Don't buy a used car without first giving it a good once-over to check for rust. Nothing can beat the old close eyeball inspection. Look everywhere, on the surface and underneath the car, for rust or signs of impending rust. Don't be afraid to bang your knuckles or run a magnet over body parts you suspect. I remember one used car in Pittsburgh that had its rocker panels replaced by hard, smooth-painted *cardboard!* It looked good, but the knuckle test discovered the coverup.

Check underneath all floor mats and trunk mats; if the car has carpeting try to get under it and inspect. Lift the spare tire and look under it. Some spares are put in wheel wells; pull the tire out and inspect the bottom of the well—this is a prime hiding place for rust. If possible, give the used car you are considering the car wash and hose leak test described above.

Keeping Rust at Bay

Frequent washing, waxing, cleaning, and visual inspections are a must if you expect your car to be rustfree.

In areas where road salts are used, be sure to hose down the underside of the car at least two or three times during the winter months. Be certain all body drain holes are open. Check the holes at the bottom of the doors to see that they are clear. After washing the car, leave all the doors open until the water has drained free; then wipe dry all the area around the inside of the door openings and around the doors themselves.

◇ ◇ ◇

A good way to flush underneath the car without getting yourself flushed is to drive the car back and forth over a sprinkler or a sprinkler hose (the kind that has numerous small holes in it). Change the position of the sprinkler or hose after every few passes of the car to ensure you get all areas clean.

◇ ◇ ◇

Periodic inspection of all areas mentioned previously will catch any moisture infiltration and nip it in the bud. Fix and seal any areas where water is finding its way in. Areas around body mouldings are particularly susceptible to rust. If small areas of surface rust are found they can be sanded clean, primed with a rustproof primer or treated with a chemical rust inhibitor, and then repainted.

◇ ◇ ◇

Any road badges—scrapes, scratches, stone chips, and the like— should be cleaned, dried, repaired, and repainted as soon as possible. Exposed bare metal is the favorite target of rust.

Odds and Ends

There is a strong relationship between extended automobile life and better gas mileage. Anything you do to increase mileage will also have a beneficial effect on engine life, and most anything you do to prolong engine life will pay off in a bonus of more miles per gallon. When you take your car in for a tune-up, you rightfully expect to get better mileage and performance after the tune-up is completed. You may not expect to get extended engine life thrown in, but anything done to make the engine more efficient will make it last longer. An oil change at the proper time helps keep the engine clean and allows it to function longer—it also lets the engine run more efficiently so you get better mpg's. Although there are exceptions to the mileage–engine life relationship, it is a good general rule to keep in mind.

◇ ◇ ◇

Fix the small things as they occur—don't put them off. If a bulb or a fuse burns out, replace it; if you spill something on the rug, clean it; if the car has just been driven over muddy or dusty roads, wash it. Don't let the car "get ahead of you." Fix or perform services when required and you'll keep the car looking younger and running longer. Fixing the little things immediately was the credo of all of the 100,000+ -mile car owners mentioned at the beginning of the book.

Another plus in having a car last a long time is that you can take advantage of the many lifetime-guarantee automotive products now available. Lifetime batteries, mufflers, shock absorbers, wheel alignment and balancing packages, and the like are all contingent upon your keeping the car they were installed in or performed on. Just this alone can mean considerable savings for you, given the fact that nothing gets cheaper anymore.

WARNING! Although these items may indeed be good deals for the longevity-minded consumer who has no desire to purchase another vehicle, they also can be loss-leader or come-on bait to get you into the service center or repair shop. Once there you may be told other work is needed. Be absolutely certain that what is proposed is actually something you need. Sure, you may save some money on the free lifetime replacement part, but you could lose much more if you're prodded into buying service or parts you don't need.

In a booklet on fuel economy I did for the State of Arizona, two stickers are included, one for the bumper or rear window and one for the dash. The rear bumper sticker reads "I SAVE GAS," while the dash sticker says "THINK ECONOMY." The bumper sticker lets your neighbor know that you are driving economically; the dash sticker prods and reminds you to do so. This is a good idea for car life also. Print the words "THINK ECONOMY" on a piece of paper and tape it to your dash in a conspicuous place. You'll be surprised how much it helps, because it acts as a constant reminder for you to watch your driving and to be prudent during the cold start. Other words or slogans will do just as nicely. "LONG LIVE MY CAR" and "THIS BABY COSTS 15 GRAND" may be excellent reminders to take it easy and follow the suggestions outlined herein.

If you'd like up to five free "Think Economy" pressure-sensitive stickers, send a stamped self-addressed envelope to: The Mileage Company, P.O. Box 40063, Tucson, AZ 85717.

The telephone can add many effective days to your car's lifespan. How? By doing as Ma Bell says: Let your fingers do the walking and you do the talking *before* you start on that trip. Many needless trips can be avoided this way—for example, by consolidating what may have been two or three separate trips into one. Call first, make sure the place of business is open or the person is at home before you start out. One less trip now means one more that can be made in the future. Any time you eliminate a trip, especially one of five miles or less with a cold engine, the car benefits dramatically, and so does our air.

One of the best ways to extend your car's life is to join a carpool. Carpooling with three other drivers means you use the car only one-fourth as much as you would if you drove to work alone. True, you may not be extending the actual total mileage potential of your car, *but you are extending the total time it will last*. Most cities now have computer matching services available for those wanting to carpool or vanpool. It will pay you to join, not only for the gas you save but for the reduced wear and tear on the car and on yourself.

A car is meant to be your servant and not the other way around. You should keep in mind, though, that the servants who perform best are the ones who are clothed and fed well and provided with adequate shelter. Your car is no different.

Have you ever noticed that the owners who tend to keep their cars a long time always seem to have names for their cars? Those "Old Faithfuls" and little "Putt-Putts" never seem to quit running. Now giving your car a name may not help it last longer, but who knows? It sure can't do any harm!

This book has provided you with the most up-to-date information available on how to make your car run more efficiently and safely, get better fuel economy, and last a lot longer. These are indeed admirable goals. Over the long run their implementation will save you money by reducing operating costs and repairs and will allow for a better resale value. But perhaps the most rewarding aspect of intensive preventive maintenance is one most car owners overlook. Each time you do something to make your car last or get better fuel economy—use of high-quality gasolines, frequent oil changes, tune-ups, efficient driving habits—you help contribute to cleaner air and a better environment.

We can't do without our cars. But we can drive them and maintain them in a fashion that lessens their negative impact on our environment. Just about every tip in this book will help. A car run at peak efficiency produces a minimal amount of pollutants. That means that our air and environment will be just a bit cleaner than they would be otherwise. It's something every car owner should keep in mind.

In the past the rewards of keeping a car up were measured, as I have mentioned, in dollars saved and a better-running and safer car. But I believe it has now become our *responsibility* to keep our cars going as efficiently as possible; it shouldn't be a choice anymore.

The way we treat our cars today will have a direct impact on the quality of life tomorrow. With *Drive It Forever* you have taken an important step, not only in making your car last longer and run better, but in helping insure a cleaner, more pollutant-free environment. And when you look at it, that may be the most important benefit of all.

If you liked *Drive It Forever* and would like to have information of

For more information about automobile longevity, and "moly" products, send a stamped self-addressed long envelope to:

THE MILEAGE COMPANY
P.O. Box 40063
Tucson, Arizona 85717

this sort on a weekly basis, check your local newspaper for my syndicated column "Drive It Forever." If your paper doesn't carry it, ask the newspaper's editor to contact the New York Times Syndication Sales Corporation for details.

Notes

Chapter 1

9   Figure 1: "A Study of the Technological Improvements in Automobile Fuel Consumption," U.S. Department of Transportation, 1975.

10   Figure 2: Ibid.

14–18   Illustrations and material on these pages adapted from Bob Allen, "Improved Vehicle Efficiency," McDonnell Douglas Corp., Long Beach, California, 1977.

19–20   Illustrations and material on these pages adapted from William Gruse, *Motor Oils: Performance and Evaluation*, Litton Educational Publishing, New York, 1967.

Chapter 2

27   Robert Sikorsky, *How to Get More Miles per Gallon*, St. Martin's Press, New York, 1978.

31   *Motor Oils.*

32   Ibid.

34   *How to Get More Miles per Gallon.*

Chapter 3

43   Figure 12. *Motor Oil Guide*, American Petroleum Institute, Publication 1551, 5th Edition, 1976.

66–67   Ibid.

67   Ibid.

Chapter 4

70–71   *Motor Oil Guide.*

74   Figure 15. Eric R. Braithwaite, Lubrication and Lubricants, Elsevier Scientific Publishing, Amsterdam, 1967.

78   *Motor Oil Guide.*

80–81   Ibid.

Chapter 5

93   *How to Get More Miles per Gallon.*
95   D.R. Blackmore and A. Thomas, *Fuel Economy of the Gasoline Engine,* John Wiley and Sons, New York, and Macmillan, London and Basingstoke, 1977.
95   Figure 16. Ibid.

Chapter 6

102–106   Illustrations and material on these pages adapted from *Fuel Economy of the Gasoline Engine.*

Chapter 7

124   *Lubrication and Lubricants.*
130   Ibid.
131   Figure 19, Ibid.
138–139   Figures 22 and 23. *Fuel Economy of the Gasoline Engine.*

Chapter 8

146   *How to Get More Miles per Gallon.*
147   Figure 24. "A Study of the Technological Improvements in Automobile Fuel Consumption."
158   *How to Get More Miles per Gallon.*
159   Figure 25. Bob Allen, *Vehicular Energy Conservation Program,* McDonnell Douglas Corp., Long Beach, California.
160–161   *Lubrication and Lubricants.*
165   *Fuel Economy of the Gasoline Engine.*

Chapter 10

174–175   *Lubrication and Lubricants.*
176   Ibid.

Index